Achieving World-Class Education in Brazil

© 2012 The International Bank for Reconstruction and
Development / The World Bank
1818 H Street NW
Washington DC 20433
Telephone: 202-473-1000
Internet: www.worldbank.org

All rights reserved

1 2 3 4   15 14 13 12

This volume is a product of the staff of the International Bank for Reconstruction and Development / The World Bank. The findings, interpretations, and conclusions expressed in this volume do not necessarily reflect the views of the Executive Directors of The World Bank or the governments they represent.

The World Bank does not guarantee the accuracy of the data included in this work. The boundaries, colors, denominations, and other information shown on any map in this work do not imply any judgement on the part of The World Bank concerning the legal status of any territory or the endorsement or acceptance of such boundaries.

Rights and Permissions
The material in this publication is copyrighted. Copying and/or transmitting portions or all of this work without permission may be a violation of applicable law. The International Bank for Reconstruction and Development / The World Bank encourages dissemination of its work and will normally grant permission to reproduce portions of the work promptly.

For permission to photocopy or reprint any part of this work, please send a request with complete information to the Copyright Clearance Center Inc., 222 Rosewood Drive, Danvers, MA 01923, USA; telephone: 978-750-8400; fax: 978-750-4470; Internet: www.copyright.com.

All other queries on rights and licenses, including subsidiary rights, should be addressed to the Office of the Publisher, The World Bank, 1818 H Street NW, Washington, DC 20433, USA; fax: 202-522-2422; e-mail: pubrights@worldbank.org.

ISBN: 978-0-8213-8854-9
eISBN: 978-0-8213-8855-6
DOI: 10.1596/978-0-8213-8854-9

Library of Congress Cataloging-in-Publication data have been requested.

Cover photo: © erproductions/Blend Images/Corbis

Achieving World-Class Education in Brazil

The Next Agenda

Barbara Bruns, David Evans and Javier Luque

Contents

Foreword		*ix*
Acknowledgments		*xi*
About the Authors		*xiii*
Abbreviations		*xiv*
Executive Summary		*xvii*

Chapter 1: Brazilian Education 1995–2010: Transformation — 1
- Education Finance Reform — 4
- Measuring Results — 7
- Reducing Schooling Costs for Poor Children — 8
- Federal Oversight — 11
- Conclusion — 12

Chapter 2: Brazilian Basic Education: Meeting the Challenge? — 15
- Meeting the Needs of a 21st Century Economy — 15
- Reducing Inequality and Poverty — 31
- Transforming Spending into Learning — 40
- Conclusion — 52

Chapter 3: Brazilian Basic Education 2011–2021: The Next Agenda — 55
- Building Better Teachers — 55
- Strengthening Early Childhood Education — 76

Schooling a 21st Century Workforce:
Raising Quality in Secondary Education ... 85
Maximizing Federal Impact and Capitalizing on
Brazil's Education Action Lab ... 95

References ... 103

Annex 1. **Delivering Results for Children in Rio's Favelas: Escola Municipal Affonso Varzea** ... 109

Annex 2. **Delivering Results for Children in Northeast Brazil: Pernambuco Escola Estadual Tomé Francisco** ... 113

Annex 3. **Access to and Quality of Early Childhood Development in Brazil Compared with the OECD and LAC Countries** ... 117

Annex 4. **Global Evidence on Universal Versus Targeted Early Childhood Development Coverage** ... 123

Annex 5. **Skills Composition in the Brazilian Labor Market** ... 127

Annex 6. **Tables** ... 135

Boxes
1. Avoiding Perverse Incentives: Brazil's Index of Basic Educational Quality ... 9
2. Basic Numeracy as Measured on PISA ... 21
3. Evaluating the Impact of São Paulo's Prova de Promoção ... 60
4. Holding Teachers Accountable for Performance: Washington D.C.'s IMPACT Program ... 71
5. The U.S. Race to the Top Program ... 101

Figures
1. Primary Education Enrollment by Provider, 1990–2009 ... 5
2. FUNDEF/FUNDEB Expenditures, 1998–2010 ... 7
3. Cognitive Skills and Economic Growth Across Regions ... 17
4. Cognitive Skills and Economic Growth Across Countries ... 17
5. PISA 2009 Math Scores, All Countries ... 19
6. Brazil's PISA Math Performance, 2000–2009 ... 20
7. Comparative PISA Math Proficiency, 2009 ... 22
8. Math Proficiency on SAEB/Prova Brasil, 1995–2009 ... 23

9.	Share of Students by Proficiency Level, Reading and Math, PISA 2000–2009	24
10.	Change in Average Educational Attainment in Brazil, 1993–2009	26
11.	Shifts in Real Wages for Workers by Years of Schooling, 1993–2009	27
12.	Changing Demand for Skills in the U.S. Economy, 1959–1999	28
13.	Changes in Brazil's Occupational Structure, 1980–2009	29
14.	Evolution of Skills in the Labor Force: United States and Brazil, 1981–2009	30
15.	Skills Evolution in the Top Two Quintiles of the Brazilian Labor Force, 1981–2009	31
16.	Regional Trends in Educational Attainment, 1993–2009	33
17.	Educational Attainment by Region, 2009	33
18.	Educational Attainment for Urban and Rural Populations, 2009	34
19.	Fourth-Grade Math Performance by Region, 1999–2009	35
20.	Educational Attainment of 20-Year-Olds Compared with Their Household Heads, 1993–2009	35
21.	Years of Schooling Completed and PISA Math Performance by Household Income Quintile	36
22.	Cost-Effectiveness of Alternative Education Programs	40
23.	Consolidated Education Spending, 2000–2009	41
24.	Public Expenditure on Education as a Percentage of GDP in OECD Countries and Brazil, 2007	42
25.	Projected Evolution of Schooling Cohorts, 1990–2025	43
26.	Spending per Student at Different Levels Relative to Unit Costs in Primary Education, 2007	46
27.	Average Class Size by Level of Education, 2008	49
28.	Comparative PISA Math Performance of Prospective Teachers and Engineers	57
29.	Cognitive Development of Children Aged 36–72 Months in Ecuador	77
30.	Distribution of Crèches and Preschools in Brazil by Quality	82

Tables

1.	Average Years of Schooling Completed by the Adult Population in Selected Countries, 1960–2010	2
2.	Secondary Education Gross Enrollment Ratio in Selected Countries, 1990–2008	3

3.	FUNDEB-Mandated 2010 Spending Levels	6
4.	Expansion of Bolsa Escola/Bolsa Família, 2002–2009	11
5.	Brazilian Basic Education 2009 - Key Statistics	13
6.	Average Real Wages by Years of Schooling, 1993-2009	26
7.	Projected Declines in Schooling Cohorts, 2010–2025	44
8.	A New Model of Highly Selective Recruitment: Teach For All Programs in Latin America	63
9.	Use of Class Time: Rio de Janeiro, Pernambuco, and Minas Gerais	66
10.	Use of Classroom Materials: Rio de Janeiro, Pernambuco, and Minas Gerais	66
11.	Students Off-Task: Rio de Janeiro, Pernambuco, and Minas Gerais	67
12.	Use of Instructional Time in Top versus Bottom Performing Rio de Janeiro Municipal Schools, 2010	67
13.	Student Engagement in Top versus Bottom Performing Rio de Janeiro Municipal Schools, 2010	68
14.	Classroom Dynamics in 220 Pernambuco Schools, November 2009	75
15.	Improvements in Access to Early Childhood Education in Brazil, 1996–2009	79
16.	Early Childhood Education Training in Denmark, France, and Sweden, 2000	84
17.	Share of Secondary Enrollment at Night in State Schools and IDEB Ranking, 2009	86
18.	Distribution of Secondary Enrollment by Type of School and Shift, and PISA Math Scores, 2009	88

Foreword

Education is improving in Brazil. We can see it in the coverage: the average years of education has almost doubled over the last 20 years, as has the proportion of adults who have completed secondary school. We can also see it in the quality, albeit more modestly: Brazil's high school students have improved consistently in math and language performance over the last decade. These gains stem from the federal government's priority attention to education through both reforms and resources over the past 15 years. The progress laid out in this book is impressive and praiseworthy, but Brazil still trails its competitors in several of the ways that matter most. Student learning, while improving, still lags far behind wealthier nations. Many secondary schools lose the majority of their students well before graduation. Teachers are drawn from among the lowest achievers and have few performance incentives, and it shows in how class time is used.

This important book explores not only the basis for Brazil's progress, but also what it must do to bridge the remaining quality gap to a first-rate education for its children. It provides detailed recommendations for strengthening the performance of teachers, supporting children's early development, and reforming secondary education. In Brazil's highly decentralized basic education system, each level of government has an integral role to play.

The World Bank recognizes the vital nature of investments in human capital for the long-term well-being of Brazil's citizens and its economy. This education report is part of a broad program of World Bank analytical work on Brazil's investments in people. Another recently released study *(Becoming Old in an Older Brazil: Implications of Population Aging on Growth, Poverty, Public Finance and Service Delivery)* traces the projected rise of the elderly in Brazil from 11 percent of the total population in 2005 to 49 percent in 2050, and the substantial economic and social changes this will trigger. A forthcoming study focuses on Brazil's youngest generation, and the challenge of ensuring all children the early education, health and nutrition support they need to protect and realize their full human potential. A further study examines jobs and productivity in Brazil, how recent government policies and economic trends have affected the quality of work for Brazilians, and how the right policies to support on-the-job training can strengthen ongoing human capital investments. The World Bank will continue to work closely with the Government of Brazil to bring international experience and state-of-the-art research to finding the best solutions to Brazil's policy challenges.

I hope that policy makers across Brazil will read *Achieving World-Class Education in Brazil* and consider the analysis and policy suggestions it provides. It puts the very best research and statistics on education in Brazil into global perspective, accessible language, and a digestible length. It aims to support Brazil's continued commitment to education, and therefore to the Brazilian economy and people of the future. As Brazil's population ages, finding resources to invest in the young will prove increasingly difficult. The time for giant strides towards world-class education is now.

Makhtar Diop
Country Director for Brazil
The World Bank

Acknowledgments

This report reflects the work of a large World Bank team and a much larger set of government, academic, and nongovernmental organization (NGO) partners in Brazil who have guided and supported our efforts. Invaluable research funding was provided by the Spanish Impact Evaluation Fund (SIEF) and the Bank-Netherlands Partnership Program (BNPP).

We thank first of all the policy makers who are, day in and day out, reshaping education systems in Brazil to give more chances to poor children and to produce the skilled and educated citizens the country needs for success in the 21st century. These education leaders and their teams have been generous with their time, open with information, and insightful with their suggestions and guidance. They include Minister Fernando Haddad, Executive Secretary Henrique Paim, Basic Education Secretary Maria do Pilar Lacerdo Almeida e Silva, and Leonardo Osvaldo Barchini Rosa of the Brazilian Ministry of Education; former director Elaine Pazello, Gabriela Moriconi, and Nuzyare Almeida at the National Institute for Education Studies and Research; former secretaries Danilo Cabral and Nilton Mota, and Margareth Zaponi, Epifânia Godoy Valenca, Henriette Medeiros, and Ezyneide Cavalcanti of the Pernambuco State Education Secretariat; former Minas Gerais state education secretary Vanessa Guimarães, and current state secretary Ana Lucia Gazzola, former executive secretary João Filocre, and Raquel Santos, Sônia Andere, Juliana Riani, Rafael Morais, Guilherme Rosa and Hilda Pochman; Rio de Janeiro municipal education secretary Claudia Costin and Helena Bomeny, Jurema Holperin, Luiza Vaz, Teca Pontual, Eduardo de Pádua

Nazar, Rafael Parente and Luiz Eduardo Conde; Rio de Janeiro state education secretary Wilson Risolia and Sônia Barone, Mirela de Carvalho, Alyne Satos, Reinaldo Ferreira and Antonio Lousao; former Acre state education secretary Maria Correa da Silva and Francisca das Chagas; and Camila Barros of the São Paulo State Education Secretariat.

A very special thanks goes to director Eliane Sampaio and professor Fabiana Dutra of the Escola Municipal Affonso Varzea in Rio de Janeiro, who opened their school and their homes so our team could produce the profile in annex 1; and to director Ivan Jose Nunes Francisco and professor Angela Maria de Oliveira of the Escola Estadual Tomé Francisco in Pernambuco, who did the same for the profile in annex 2.

The classroom observation data in this report would not have been possible without the technical support of Audrey Moore and Elizabeth Adelman of the Academy for Educational Development, Datamétrica's Alexandre Rands and André Magalhães and their team, and the Instituto Hartman Regueira in Minas Gerais.

New evidence from impact evaluations is thanks to the intellectual leadership of Professor Claudio Ferraz of the Pontifical Catholic University of Rio de Janeiro, and outstanding research support from Tassia Cruz and Vitor Pereira. We also benefited greatly from the knowledge and guidance of Guiomar de Mello, Rose Neubauer da Silva, Claudio de Moura Castro, Ricardo Paes de Barros, Simon Schwartzman, Mirela de Carvalho, Jorge Werthein, Laudo Bernardes, Bernadette Gatti, Maria Malta Campos, Anna Helena Altenfelder, Ana Lucia Kassouf, Viviane Senna, Ilona Becskeházy, Paula Louzano, Katrina Kosec, and W. Steven Barnett.

This report would not have been possible without the efforts of contributing members of the research team Erica Amorim, Debora Brakarz, Tassia Cruz, Madalena dos Santos, Luciana Harrington, Martin Moreno, and Vitor Pereira, nor without the administrative support of Marize Santos. At the outset and all along the way, our team benefited enormously from the comments and guidance of peer reviewers Maria Helena Guimarães de Castro, Naercio Menezes Filho, Sajitha Bashir, and Alberto Rodriguez and colleagues Chingboon Lee, Tito Cordella, Michele Gragnolati, Mauro Azeredo, Francisco Ferreira, and Laura Chioda.

Above all, we are grateful to Makhtar Diop for inspiring and supporting this study, which—in its emphasis on generating new data and evidence from rigorous impact evaluations in Brazil—represents a new type of analytical work for the World Bank.

Finally, with gratitude and sadness, we acknowledge the advice and support of former Education Minister Paulo Renato Souza throughout the preparation of this report. Paulo Renato's imprint on Brazilian education cannot be overstated. The fifteen years of educational progress recounted in this volume is in large measure his legacy.

About the Authors

Barbara Bruns is lead economist in the Latin America and the Caribbean Region of the World Bank, responsible for education. She is currently leading a multi-year research study of teacher quality in Latin America and co-managing several impact evaluations of teacher pay for performance reforms in Brazil. She is co-author of the book *Making Schools Work: New Evidence on Accountability Reforms* (2011, with Deon Filmer and Harry Patrinos). As the first manager of the $14 million Spanish Impact Evaluation Fund (SIEF) at the World Bank from 2007 to 2009, Barbara oversaw the launch of more than 50 rigorous impact evaluations of health, education, and social protection programs. She also co-authored the World Bank/IMF MDG Global Monitoring Reports of 2005, 2006 and 2007, served on the UN Secretary General's Education Task force in 2003, and co-authored the book *A Chance for Every Child: Achieving Universal Primary Education by 2015* (2003). From 2002-2004, she headed the Secretariat of the global Education for All Fast Track Initiative (EFA FTI). She holds degrees from the London School of Economics and the University of Chicago.

David Evans is an economist in the Human Development Department of the Latin America and the Caribbean Region. He joined the World Bank in 2007 as Co-Coordinator of the Africa Program of Education Impact Evaluations, and has designed and managed rigorous evaluations of education projects in Brazil, Mexico, Haiti, the Gambia, Kenya, Sierra Leone, and Tanzania, on topics including the impact of school uniform provision, conditional cash transfers, school grants, school management training, teacher training, and textbook provision. He is co-author of *Early Child Education: Making Programs Work for Brazil's Most Important Generation* (2011), is co-managing a randomized impact evaluation of Rio de Janeiro's day care system, as well as leading a regional ECD Community of Practice, linking professionals across sectors and countries in Latin America. Prior to joining the World Bank, David was a researcher at the RAND corporation. He holds a PhD in economics from Harvard University.

Javier Luque is a Senior Education Economist in the Latin America and Caribbean Region of the World Bank. He has published extensively on education and labor market issues, across different countries in Latin America and East Asia. He has also worked as a policy maker. Before joining the World Bank, he held senior positions at the Central Bank of Peru and the Peruvian Ministry of Economy. Javier has also worked in the International Monetary Fund. He has held teaching positions, at undergraduate and graduate levels at the Catholic University in Peru, the University of the Pacific, San Marcos University, and the University of Rochester. He has also been a Visiting Fellow at the Center for Research on Education Outcomes (CREDO) at Stanford University's Hoover Institution. Javier Luque holds a PhD in Economics from University of Rochester (NY).

Abbreviations and Acronyms

ACS	American Community Survey
AVDI	Asignación Variable por Desempeño Individual (Individual Teacher Performance Incentive—Chile)
BDE	Bonus de Desempenho Educacional (school performance bonus—Pernambuco state)
CCT	conditional cash transfer
CEFET	Centro Federal de Educação Tecnológica (Federal Center for Technological Education)
CENPEC	Centro de Estudos em Pesquisa, Educação e Ação Comunitária (Center for Research on Education, Culture and Community Action)
CGU	Controladoria Geral da União (Brazilian Office of the Comptroller General)
ECD	early childhood development
ECERS	Early Childhood Environment Rating Scale
EDURURAL	Programa de Apoio a Educação Rural do Nordeste do Brasil (Northeast Brazil Rural Education Project—World Bank)
ENADE	Exame Nacional de Desempenho de Estudantes (National Exam for the Assessment of Student Performance)
ENEM	Exame Nacional do Ensino Médio (National Secondary Education Exit Exam)
EPI	Escola Pública Integrada (Integrated Public School)

FUNDEB	Fundo de Manutenção e Desenvolvimento da Educação Básica e de Valorização dos Profissionais da Educação (Fund for the Development of Primary Education and Appreciation of Teachers)
FUNDEF	Fundo de Desenvolvimento do Ensino Fundamental e de Valorização do Magistério (Fund for the Development of Basic Education and Appreciation of Teachers)
FUNDESCOLA	Fundo de Fortalecimento da Escola (Fund for School Strengthening and Development)
GDP	gross domestic product
ICE	Instituto de Co-responsabilidade pela Educação (Institute for Co-responsibility for Education)
ICT	information and communication technology
IDB	Inter-American Development Bank
IDEB	Índice de Desenvolvimento da Educação Básica (Index of Basic Education Development)
IDEPE	Índice de Desenvolvimento da Educação de Pernambuco (Index of Basic Education Development in Pernambuco)
IETS	Instituto de Estudos do Trabalho e Sociedade (Institute for Studies of Labor and Society)
IIIE	International Institute for Impact Evaluation
INEP	Instituto Nacional de Estudos e Pesquisas Educacionais Anísio Teixeira (Anisio Teixeira National Institute for Education Studies and Research)
ITERS	Infant/Toddler Environment Rating Scale
LAC	Latin America and the Caribbean
LDB	Lei de Diretrizes e Bases (National Basic Education Law)
MDS	Ministério do Desenvolvimento Social e Combate à Fome (Ministry of Social Development and Fight Against Hunger)
MEC	Ministério da Educação (National Ministry of Education)
MIC	middle income country
NATA	Núcleo Avançado em Tecnologia de Alimentos (Center for Advanced Food Technology)
NBER	National Bureau for Economic Research
OECD	Organisation for Economic Co-operation and Development
PAR	Plano de Ações Articuladas (Joint Action Plan)
PEP	Programa do Ensino Profissionalizante de Minas Gerais (Minas Gerais State Vocational Education Program)
PIM	Programa da Primeira Infância Melhor do Rio Grande do Sul (Rio Grande do Sul State Program for Better Early Childhood)

PIRLS	Program on International Reading Literacy Study
PISA	Program for International Student Assessment
PNAD	Pesquisa Nacional por Amostragem de Domicílios (National Household Survey—Brazil)
PPP	purchasing power parity
PROALFA	Programa de Avaliação da Alfabetização (Program to Assess Early Literacy— Minas Gerais)
PROEB	Programa de Avaliação da Educação Básica (Program to Assess Basic Education— Minas Gerais)
REDEFOR	Rede São Paulo de Formação Docente (São Paulo State Teacher Training Network)
RTT	Race to the Top
SAEB	Sistema de Avaliação da Educação Básica (National System for Evaluation of Basic Education)
SEDUC	Secretaria de Educação do Governo de Pernambuco (State Secretariat of Education of Pernambuco)
SEE	Secretaria de Estado de Educação (State Secretariat of Education)
SENAC	Serviço Nacional de Aprendizagem Comercial (National Service for Commercial Apprenticeship)
SENAI	Serviço Nacional de Aprendizagem Industrial (National Service for Industrial Apprenticeship)
SENAR	Serviço Nacional de Aprendizagem Rural (National Service for Agricultural Apprenticeship)
SIEF	Spanish Impact Evaluation Fund of the World Bank
SME	Secretaria Municipal de Educação (Municipal Secretariat of Education)
STEM	short-term economic monitor
TIMSS	Trends in International Mathematics and Science Study
UNICEF	United Nations Children's Fund

(Exchange Rate Effective September 2, 2011)

Currency Unit	=	Brazil Real (BRL)
BRL$1.00	=	US$0.61
US$1	=	BRL$1.62

FISCAL YEAR
January – December

Executive Summary

Brazil has made great strides in basic education over the past 15 years and has set audacious national goals for attaining OECD levels of quality by 2021.[1] The 2009 results for the Program for International Student Assessment (PISA), which measures high school student learning levels in more than 70 countries, confirmed Brazil's impressive progress in raising educational performance. Brazil's 52-point increase in math since 2000 indicates that students have gained a full academic year of math mastery over the decade, and the country's overall score increase—from 368 to 401—is the third largest on record. Brazil's scores still trail the averages for OECD and East Asian countries, and are no grounds for complacency. But few countries have made faster or more sustained progress.

How did Brazil move from one of the worst performing education systems of any middle-income country to strong and sustained improvement not only in learning but also in primary and secondary school coverage? What are the prospects for Brazil to achieve its goal of student learning levels on par with the OECD average over the next

---

1 Basic education in Brazil historically has consisted of a first cycle of eight grades (called primary education in this report and known as "fundamental education" in Brazil) and a second cycle of three grades (secondary education). In 2006, the country adopted legislation extending the length of compulsory schooling by one year and creating a nine-year primary cycle. The official entry age to primary school was lowered from seven to six. The preschool cycle was correspondingly shortened to cover ages four through five rather than four through six. Because the new system was not implemented until 2009, we use the old system throughout this report for consistency in comparing historical data, unless otherwise specified.

xvii

decade? What more could be done to accelerate Brazil's education advance? These are the three central questions of this report.

We focus on basic education, which is the foundation in every country for all other progress in education.[2] By telling the story of Brazil's remarkable run of policy continuity and sustained reform over the past fifteen years, we hope this report can serve as a resource for other developing countries seeking rapid progress in education. By benchmarking Brazil's current education performance in a competitive global context, we identify issues that still need attention. In reviewing the latest research from Brazil and elsewhere that can guide the design of sound reforms and cost-effective programs, we hope to stimulate and support the federal, state and municipal governments in setting the education agenda for the next decade. This report will succeed if it persuades a broad audience of Brazilian policy makers and citizens that the country is making impressive progress in education, but the agenda ahead is crucial.

The "Managed Revolution" of Brazilian Education

A six-year-old Brazilian child born today into the bottom quintile of the income distribution will complete more than twice as many years of schooling as her parents did. The rise in the average educational attainment of Brazil's labor force since 1995 has been one of the fastest on record—faster than China's. Major gaps in performance with middle-income countries in Latin America and the Caribbean and elsewhere are closing, such as in primary school completion and preschool coverage. In key areas such as assessing student learning and education performance monitoring, Brazil has become a global leader. How has Brazil accomplished this?

Chapter 1 chronicles the transformation of Brazilian education that began when the Cardoso government in 1995 assumed three critical normative functions at the federal level that had previously gone unfilled. These were: (1) equalizing funding across regions, states and municipalities with the FUNDEF reform; (2) measuring the learning of all children on a common national yardstick (SAEB); and (3) protecting the educational opportunity of students from poor families (Bolsa Escola). With those reforms, plus the first comprehensive legal framework for basic education (the Lei de Diretrizes e Bases de Educação, or National Basic Education Law, in 1996) and the first national curriculum guidelines, the Ministry of Education got the core elements of a national education policy profoundly right.

---

2   Two earlier World Bank publications—*Higher Education in Brazil: Challenges and Options (2002)* and *Knowledge and Innovation for Competitiveness in Brazil (2008)*—focused on higher education.

But what happened next was equally important. The Lula da Silva administration, elected in 2002, not only retained these core policies but expanded and strengthened them. FUNDEF financing equalization was extended to secondary schools and preschools. Bolsa Escola was consolidated with other transfer programs into Bolsa Familia, and coverage grew from 8.2 million students in 2002 to 17.7 million in 2009, with cash transfers increasing from 3.4 to 11.9 billion reais. The testing of a small national sample of students every two years under SAEB was extended to a nationwide test of math and Portuguese called Prova Brasil, and applied to all 4th, 8th, and 11th grade students. The results were combined with data on student enrollment, repetition, and graduation rates to generate a comprehensive index of school performance, the Index of Basic Education Development (IDEB). With an IDEB score for all but the smallest of Brazil's 175,000 primary and secondary schools, 5,000-plus municipal school systems, 26 state systems, and the federal district, every segment of the Brazilian education system can benchmark how well its students are learning and how efficiently its school or school system is performing. No other large federal country has achieved this level of assessment.

Federal, state, and municipal policies in education have been progressive and innovative in other areas as well. The Ministry of Education's strong normative role has included new standards for teachers; high-quality federally supported teacher training programs; and textbook screening and production. Investment support includes programs such as Mais Educação and expansion of the federal technical schools. The government has also strongly supported innovation, whether school-level planning under FUNDESCOLA (the Fund for School Strengthening and Development), multigrade teaching under Escola Ativa, or capacity building for municipal education managers. Innovative reforms have also taken hold at the state and municipal levels, which have core responsibility for the delivery of pre-primary, primary, and secondary education in Brazil.

Brazilian Education in a Competitive World

Chapter 2 examines how Brazilian education today stacks up against education in other countries in the OECD, LAC, and Asia. Brazil is moving up, but the rest of the world is not standing still. We review the performance of the education system on three paramount functions: (1) developing the labor force skills for sustained economic growth; (2) contributing to poverty and inequality reduction by providing educational opportunity for all; and (3) transforming education spending into educational results, especially student learning. We conclude that while progress has been substantial, the agenda ahead is crucial.

Labor Force Skills

Labor force skills are improving but still lag behind those in other countries. Brazil is far from achieving the average learning levels, secondary education completion rates, and student flow efficiency of OECD and other middle-income countries. Although Brazil had the strongest math improvement and third largest overall improvement (behind Luxembourg and Chile) between 2000 and 2009 on PISA, it is still not the leader in the LAC region. Chile, Uruguay, and Mexico all perform better in absolute terms. And while LAC countries as a group substantially trail the OECD average performance, the first-time entry of another BRICS (Brazil, Russia, India, China, South Africa) member into PISA (Shanghai, China) set an even higher benchmark. The gap in math skills between the average student in Shanghai and the average Brazilian student is approximately five school years. The implications are serious: over the past decade, researchers have generated compelling evidence that what counts for economic growth is what students actually learn (measured on globally benchmarked tests such as PISA) and not how many years of schooling they complete (Hanushek and Woessmann, 2007).

PISA Math Performance for Brazil and Selected Countries, 2000–2009

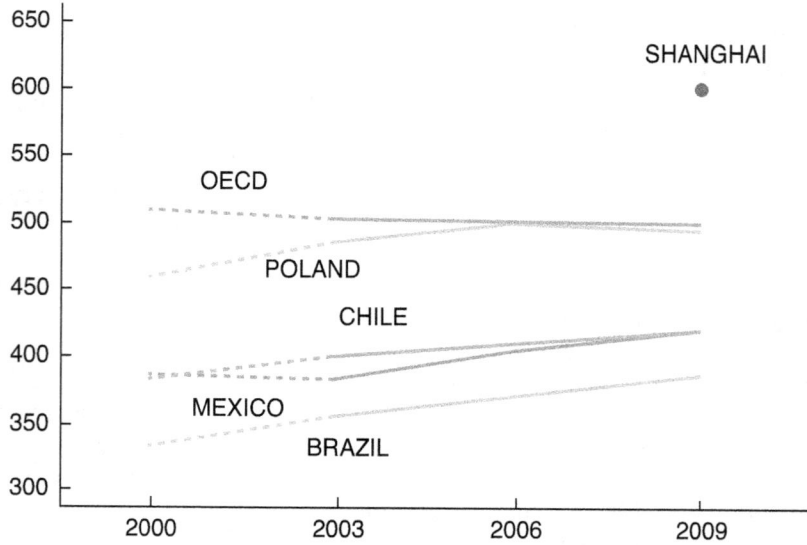

Note: The PISA math test in 2000 covered a smaller number of domains, and its results are therefore not directly comparable with the subsequent years.

The massive expansion of schooling in Brazil over the past 15 years has had dramatic effects on the labor force. In 1993, close to 70 percent of the labor force had not completed secondary school. Today that number is 40 percent. The biggest change is not access to primary school but the much higher share of children who stay in school through secondary education. The rise in the share of workers with secondary education has been accompanied by a decline in the real wage for secondary education graduates in recent years. At the same time, there has been an increase in the wage premium for higher education graduates, which is consistent with a global pattern of demand for workers with strong analytical skills. Labor market data in Brazil are signaling that 21st century skills are important for the next generation of workers. Producing graduates with these skills will be a critical challenge for the education system over the next decade—graduates with the ability to think analytically, ask critical questions, master new skills and content quickly, and operate with high-level communication/interpersonal skills, including foreign language mastery and the ability to work effectively in teams. For the basic education system, the overriding implication is the urgency of increasing student learning.

Change in Educational Attainment in Brazil, 1993-2009

(percentage of the population aged 26-30)

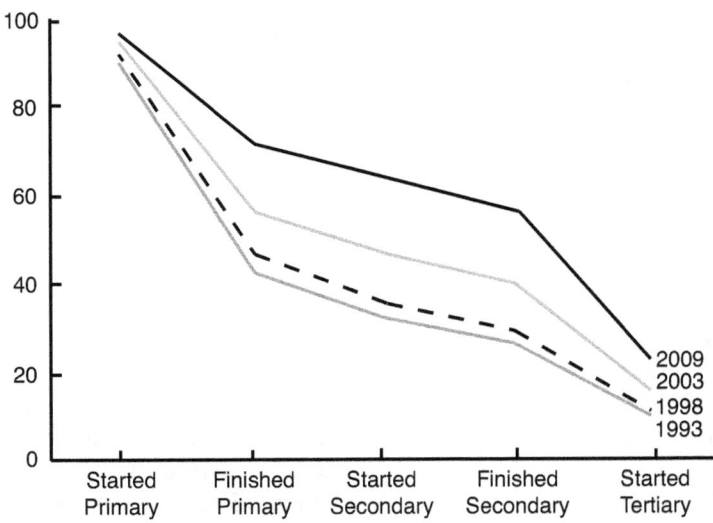

Source: PNAD, several years.

Poverty and Inequality Reduction

More equal access to education is contributing to lower inequality and poverty, but gaps in learning achievement remain. There has been a striking equalization in schooling attainment in just one generation in Brazil as a result of aggressive expansion of schooling coverage and programs such as Bolsa Familia. In 1993, the child of a father with no formal education typically completed only four years of school; today, Brazilian students complete between 9 and 11 years of schooling, regardless of their parents' educational level. The advance in education in Brazil has helped drive a significant improvement in income equality. Learning outcomes for students from the bottom income quintile have also improved, with especially rapid progress since 2006. But a gap remains.

Average Schooling Completed and PISA Learning Outcomes by Income Quintile

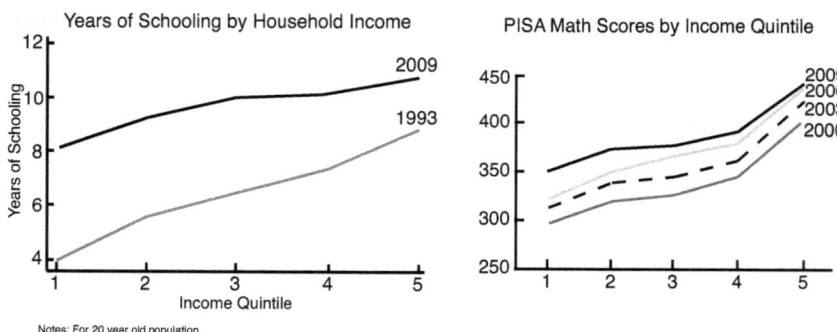

Notes: For 20 year old population

Sources: PNAD (1993, 2009); PISA data (2000-2009).

The issues underlying the low learning attainment of children from poor families have become more complex over time. Physical access to schools and household budget constraints have receded in importance, while social issues (teen pregnancy, gang and drug involvement); family instability (unemployment, domestic violence, homelessness); and learning issues and developmental deficits stemming from children's earliest years have become more prominent. Since the core equity issue in Brazilian education has shifted from equalizing access to equalizing learning attainment, secretaries of education across Brazil are increasingly focused on two major strategies, which are both consistent with global best practices: (1) targeted preventive interventions (expanding early childhood development services for low-income families), and (2) targeted remedial interventions in basic education (tutoring, accelerated learning programs, and other supports for children who are falling behind).

Efficiency of Education Spending

The report raises concerns about Brazil's current level of spending on public education, especially the government's proposed goal of raising spending to 7 percent of GDP. First, public spending on education in Brazil (5.2 percent of GDP in 2007) is already above the OECD average of 4.8 percent, which can be expected because the school-aged share of the population is larger in Brazil than in most OECD countries. However, Brazil also spends more than Mexico, Chile, India, and Indonesia, which have similar demographic profiles. Second, Brazilian GDP is growing rapidly. Third and most important, Brazil is experiencing a demographic transition that will have a dramatic impact on the school-aged population over the next decade. A projected 23 percent drop in the number of primary school students will mean almost 7 million empty seats in schools across the country. If Brazil were to follow the Korean example and hold class size constant over this period, the primary school teaching force would decline by more than 300,000 (from 1.3 million) by 2025. This

Consolidated Education Spending in Brazil and Public Education Spending As a Percentage of GDP in OECD and Selected Developing Countries

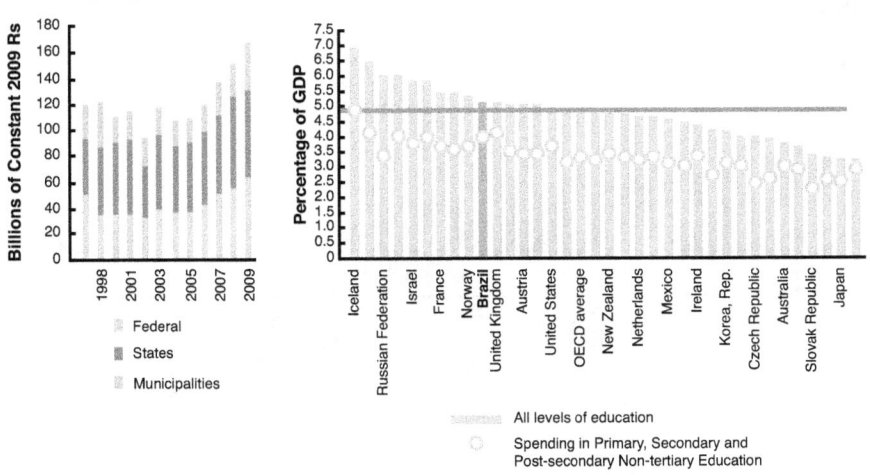

Source: Brazilian National Treasury.   *Source:* OECD (2010, table B2.4).

transition is a bonus for the education system and would permit more selectivity in teacher recruitment and a large increase in schooling quality at current spending levels.

The pursuit of spending increases should not detract attention from areas in which comparative data show that Brazil's current level of spending should be producing better results. One of these is the allocation of public funds across different levels of education: while OECD countries spend, on average, twice as much per student in tertiary education as at the primary level, Brazil spends almost six times as much. A second concern is persistent high repetition rates and high costs per graduate. Brazil has one of the highest repetition rates in the world, despite substantial research evidence that repetition is an ineffective strategy for raising learning. A third issue is rising teacher costs: several policies over the past decade have lowered class size and imposed across-the-board increases in teacher salaries with little evidence, either in Brazil or elsewhere, that they contribute to improved results. Fourth, while the report lauds the innovative programs, privately supported initiatives, and substantial investments in new technologies being undertaken in Brazil, we point to an almost complete lack of cost-effectiveness research to support policy makers' choices in these areas. Finally, we cite government audits and research studies that have documented a serious degree of corruption and mismanagement of education funds, and evidence that these are highly correlated with poor educational quality and results.

Spending Per Student at Different Education Levels Relative to Unit Costs in Primary Education, OECD and Selected Developing Countries, 2007

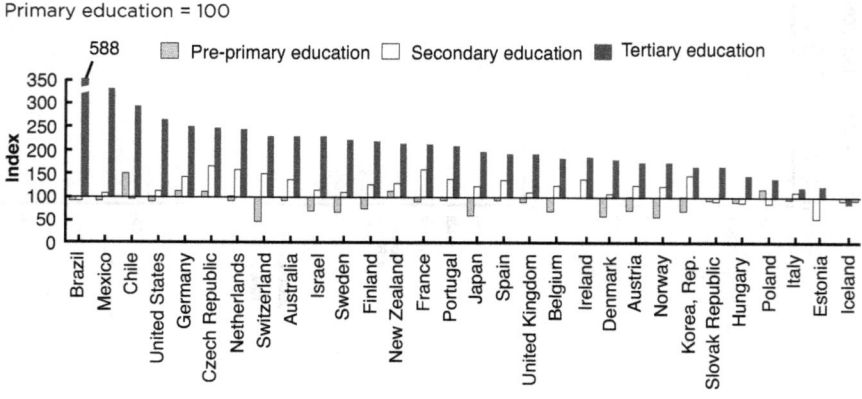

Source: OECD (2010).

Four Key Challenges for Brazilian Education, 2011-2021

Chapter 3 zeroes in on four critical challenges for the coming decade: (1) raising teacher quality; (2) protecting the early development of the most vulnerable children; (3) building a world-class secondary education system; and (4) maximizing the impact of federal policy on basic education, especially by capitalizing on the Brazilian "education action lab."

Raising Teacher Quality

In Brazil, teaching has become a low-status profession that does not attract high academic performers. Data show that teachers are recruited from the bottom third of high school students, in contrast to Singapore, Korea, and Finland, where they come from the top third. Raising teacher quality in Brazil will require recruiting higher capacity people, supporting continuous improvement in practice, and rewarding performance.

Both the federal government and some state and local governments have begun reforms in these areas; for example, teacher bonus programs (pay for performance) have been implemented in Minas Gerais, Pernambuco, and São Paulo states, and Rio de Janeiro municipality. With support from the World Bank, school systems are using standardized classroom observation methods developed in OECD countries to look inside the "black box" of the classroom and identify examples of excellent teacher practice that can anchor their professional development programs.

Use of Instructional Time in Brazil and OECD Countries

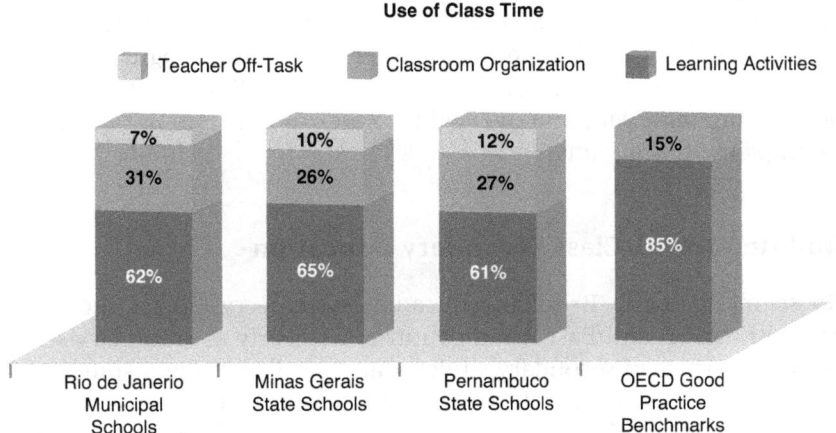

Sources: Brazilian data collected by Rio de Janeiro, Minas Gerais, and Pernambuco education secretariats during 2009 and 2010; OECD data from Abadzi (2009).

In Minas Gerais, Pernambuco, and Rio de Janeiro municipality, data show that while the OECD benchmark is 85 percent of each instructional hour effectively spent on learning activities, none of the Brazilian systems studied exceeds 66 percent.

Brazilian teachers spend substantial time on routine classroom processes, such as taking attendance and collecting papers. Many teachers also fail to use available learning materials, and students are visibly off-task between 43 percent and 64 percent of the time (in OECD countries, the benchmark for students "off-task" is 6 percent of the time or less). Instead of theory-oriented courses, teacher training programs designed as a result of classroom observation use videos and practical exercises to impart effective techniques for managing the classroom, using learning materials, and keeping students engaged and on-task. This practice-oriented teacher training is the new direction in OECD countries, and key Brazilian states and Rio de Janeiro municipality are getting ahead of the curve in this area.

Protecting Early Childhood Development

Global research points to early childhood development (ECD) interventions as the most powerful strategy for reducing inequality and leveling the education playing field. Over the past 15 years, Brazil has made progress in raising crèche enrollment from 8 percent to 18 percent of the 0–3 age group, and preschool enrollments from 49 percent to 81 percent. Priorities for the next decade are to improve the targeting of services to vulnerable low-income children and raise the quality of these services. We recommend introducing curricula tailored to each educational level; more intense training and supervision of caretakers and educators; and strengthened monitoring and evaluation of ongoing programs. In each of these areas, there is a role for the Ministry of Education (to provide orientation, materials, and oversight) as well as the state or municipality (to implement programs).

Building World-Class Secondary Education

No segment of the Brazilian education system crystallizes the quality gap with OECD and East Asian countries as clearly as secondary school. Fully 42 percent of secondary students are enrolled in night shifts, which deliver only four hours of instruction a day, compared with seven hours or more in most OECD countries and even longer school days in leading East Asian countries. Infrastructure is deplorable: the schools lack the libraries, science labs, and computer and language facilities that most

OECD students enjoy. The curriculum is overloaded and oriented toward memorization, and virtually every state secondary school system faces a severe shortage of qualified math and science teachers. As a result, 40 percent of all Brazilian secondary schools can be considered "dropout factories"—failing to graduate 60 percent of their students.

The challenges are extreme, but a number of states are working on comprehensive strategies. Some, such as Minas Gerais, are developing new approaches to a key issue for secondary education: the balance between academic and vocational content. Promising directions for improvement in secondary education in Brazil can be loosely grouped this way: systemwide strategies (curriculum and training reform, major infrastructure investments to support a longer school day and eliminate evening instruction, improving teacher quality); demonstration schools (full-day, highly resourced secondary schools that test innovations and demonstrate that high-quality secondary schools are achievable); and public-private partnerships for technical and vocational education, to ensure a smooth transition to work for secondary education graduates who do not go on to higher education by orienting the vocational content of the curriculum to skills that are in local demand and supporting more results-driven school management.

Maximizing the Federal Impact and Capitalizing on the Education Action Lab

Given the progressive, effective education policies pursued by successive federal administrations over the past 15 years, it is not easy to identify policies that could substantially speed Brazil's progress toward world-class basic education. Our analysis points to four recommendations:

- *Stay the course on the core policies of the past 15 years:* FUNDEB funding equalization, IDEB results measurement, and Bolsa Familia conditional cash transfers.

- *Focus on spending efficiency rather than targets for higher spending,* which can worsen the risks of leakage and corruption in the system.

- *Create incentives for statewide improvement.* Use more federal funding to reward states for closer integration of state and municipal school systems, and use less funding to "parachute" federal support directly to small municipal education systems.

- *Capitalize on the Brazilian "education action lab"* by supporting systematic, rigorous impact evaluation of innovative state and municipal programs.

Of these four recommendations, perhaps the last holds the most potential power. The long-term work of improving primary and secondary school performance is the responsibility of more than 5,500 state, federal district, and municipal school systems in Brazil. Literally thousands of creative new programs and policies are being tried out at this moment across Brazil by dynamic, results-oriented secretaries of education. Few other countries in the world have the scale, scope, and creativity of policy action that can be seen today in Brazil. States and municipalities are experimenting in a number of cutting-edge policy areas, using similar programs with slightly different design features, such as the pay for performance programs in Minas Gerais, São Paulo, Pernambuco, and Rio de Janeiro municipality; or the accelerated learning programs in these and other states and municipalities. The chance to study reforms and programs systematically makes Brazil one of the world's best laboratories for generating global evidence on what works in education. A concerted federal effort to mine this rich experience more effectively through rigorous impact evaluation might be the single most powerful stimulus to world-class education.

1

Brazilian Education 1995–2010: Transformation

In 1994, a six-year-old Brazilian child born into the bottom quintile of the income distribution was likely to live in the rural northeast, have a mother who had never gone to school, and complete no more than the first few grades of primary school herself, even after spending multiple years attending, locked in a cycle of repetition. The local primary school was a one- or two-room structure without electricity or water and devoid of books or materials.[3] Its teachers were usually hired through political connections with the mayor. In 60 percent of cases, the teacher had not completed secondary school; in 30 percent of cases, she had not completed primary school. On unannounced visits, teachers and students might not be found in the school at all; when education researchers evaluating the World Bank's Northeast Rural Education Project in the late 1980s revisited their sample of 600 primary schools across three states, over 30 percent of them had ceased to function (Harbison and Hanushek 1992, p. 39).

Schooling access and quality were less precarious in larger cities and richer parts of the country. Still, in 1990 Brazil lagged far behind middle-income Latin American and Caribbean (LAC) countries and dramatically trailed OECD countries on every imaginable educational indicator. Less than 40 percent of children nationally completed the eight grades of primary school, compared with 70 percent for the LAC region and 95 percent for the OECD.[4] Only 38 percent of children enrolled in secondary

---

3 In 1992, the federal textbook agency distributed 8.8 million textbooks, less than 10 percent of the estimated 100 million required for the 30 million primary and secondary students.
4 As noted previously, unless otherwise specified in this report, we use pre-2009

school, compared with over 70 percent in Argentina and Chile, and 91 percent across the OECD. The average schooling level of the labor force in 1990 was 3.8 years—less than half that of Argentina, Chile, and the OECD (see table 1). Fewer than 20 percent of primary teachers in Brazil had a higher education degree. Teacher wages in many rural areas were less than half the minimum wage. There were no national data on student learning.

Fast forward to 2010. A six-year-old in the bottom quintile of the income distribution today will go on to complete more than twice as many years of schooling as her parents. No matter where in the country her school is located, per student spending will be protected at a level adequate for desks, electricity, water, books, pencils, and workbooks. Her teacher will have at least a secondary school degree, and 60 percent of teachers nationally have higher education credentials. No matter where a school is located, its teachers will earn at least 1,000 Rs per month, twice

---

nomenclature (e.g., fourth grade, eighth grade) rather than the new nomenclature (e.g., fifth year, ninth year) to analyze historical trends in the data.

Table 1. Average Years of Schooling Completed by the Adult Population in Selected Countries, 1960–2010

	1960	1990	2000	2010	Ratio 2010/1990	2010/1960
Argentina	5.3	7.9	8.6	9.3	1.2	1.7
Brazil	1.8	3.8	5.6	7.2	1.9	4.0
Chile	5.0	8.1	8.8	9.7	1.2	1.9
Colombia	2.8	5.5	6.5	7.3	1.3	2.6
Mexico	2.6	5.5	7.4	8.5	1.5	3.3
Peru	3.2	6.6	7.7	8.7	1.3	2.7
Canada	8.1	10.3	11.1	11.5	1.1	1.4
France	4.1	7.1	9.3	10.4	1.5	2.5
United Kingdom	6.0	7.9	8.5	9.3	1.2	1.5
USA	8.9	12.3	13.0	12.4	1.0	1.4
China	1.4	4.9	6.6	7.5	1.6	5.2
Japan	7.2	9.9	10.7	11.5	1.2	1.6
Korea, Rep.	3.2	8.9	10.6	11.6	1.3	3.6
OECD average	6.1	8.9	9.9	10.7	1.2	1.7

Source: Barro-Lee (2010).

Table 2. Secondary Education Gross Enrollment Ratio in Selected Countries, 1990–2008

(total students enrolled as percentage of the relevant age group)

	1990	2000	2008	Ratio 2008/1990
Argentina	71	86	85*	1.2
Brazil	38	104	101	2.6
Chile	73	83	91*	1.2
Colombia	50	69	91	1.8
Mexico	53	72	90	1.7
Peru	67	87	89	1.3
Canada	101	107	100**	1.0
France	98	110	113	1.1
United Kingdom	88	102	99	1.1
United States	92	94	94	1.0
China	49	63	76	1.6
Japan	97	102	101	1.0
Korea, Rep.	90	94	97	1.1
OECD average	91	108	105	1.1

* 2007, ** 2006

Sources: Barro-Lee (2000 and updates); www.unesco.org.

the minimum salary. Perhaps the most significant change of all is that the school system at all levels knows how much that child is learning.

As the result of a remarkable 15-year run of policy continuity and sustained reform, the 2009 PISA results confirmed that Brazil has made substantial progress in education. This report lays out the substantial agenda ahead, but there is no question that Brazil's efforts over the past 15 years are bearing fruit. From 1990 through 2010, Brazil's increase in the educational attainment of the labor force was one of the fastest on record, and faster than that of China. Secondary school enrollments in Brazil have grown faster and are now higher than in any other LAC country, although part of this ratio reflects high repetition (table 2). Other major gaps in performance are also closing, such as in primary school completion and preschool coverage. In key areas such as assessing student learning and educational performance monitoring, Brazil in 2010 is not only the leader in the LAC region but a global model.

What has driven this advance? There have been many innovations in education policy over the past 15 years at the federal, state, and municipal levels, and this report highlights a number of them. But the most important forces behind Brazil's progress are in three critical areas where national policy has been on par with global best practice and implementation has been sustained and effective:

- Education finance equalization
- Results measurement
- Conditional cash transfers to increase schooling attainment of the poor.

Education Finance Reform

The transformation of the federal government role in education finance in Brazil over the past 15 years is the revolutionary change that made all other progress possible. Before the creation of the basic education equalization fund, FUNDEF (Fundo de Desenvolvimento do Ensino Fundamental) in 1996, wide disparities in spending per student existed across regions in Brazil and across school providers within regions. The 1988 constitution had devolved responsibility for crèche and preschool services to municipalities and secondary education to states, but primary education was a divided responsibility between states and municipalities. The national landscape was an administratively confused welter of state and municipal schools that were geographically proximate but had very different levels of per student resources and quality. The constitution required that 25 percent of all state and municipal taxes and transfers be spent on education, but the mandate did not take account of the large variations in both schooling coverage and tax revenues across jurisdictions. As a result, while spending per primary student in municipal schools in parts of northeast Brazil was less than Rs 100 per year (lower than in Nicaragua and Bolivia), it could be Rs 600 or more in state schools in the same region and Rs 1,500 or more in state and municipal systems in the southeast (on par with schools in Korea and Singapore).

FUNDEF addressed these disparities through a threefold strategy. First, it guaranteed a national minimum level of spending per student in primary education, which was set at Rs 315 in 1998, FUNDEF's first year of implementation. This represented a significant increase in resources for primary students in the northeast, north, and center west states—especially in municipal schools. The guaranteed capitation level meant that funding would follow the student, which created a significant incentive for school systems—especially underfunded municipal systems—to expand their enrollments. After 1998, municipalities instituted school bus systems, enrollment campaigns, school feeding, and other inducements to get children into school for the first time. There was a significant increase in overall primary enrollments, with the net enrollment ratio in the northeast and north climbing from 77 percent and 82 percent, respectively, to 94 percent by 2008; and there was a large overall shift in primary enrollment from state to municipal schools (figure 1).

Funding could follow the student because of FUNDEF's second feature: a federally mandated system of redistribution within states and a federally managed top-up fund, supplemented with federal resources. States were required to share resources across municipalities so that all state and municipal schools within the state could achieve the mandated per student spending threshold. The federal fund redistributed fiscal resources to states that were unable to achieve the threshold through their own tax revenues. Overnight in 1998, FUNDEF redistributed Rs 30.6 billion (25 percent of total primary education spending) to six states. On average, FUNDEF tops up education resources annually for 6 of Brazil's 26 states (and federal district).

FUNDEF's third key feature was a mandate that 60 percent of the total per student allocation be spent on teacher salaries and 40 percent on other operating costs. States and municipalities were free to spend above the

Figure 1. Primary Education Enrollment by Provider, 1990-2009

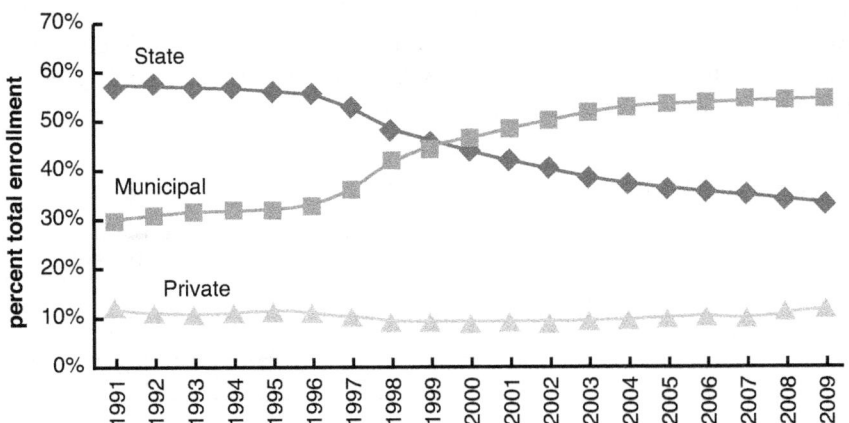

Sources: National Institute for Education Studies and Research/ Brazilian Ministry of Education (INEP/MEC).

federally established floor, and many did. But the impact of the mandate in its first several years was a 70 percent increase in average teacher salaries in poorer municipalities in the northeast and north (Gordon and Vegas 2005).

FUNDEF included a sunset clause after eight years. One of the most important examples of policy continuity between the Cardoso and Lula da Silva administrations was the reauthorization and expansion of FUNDEF in 2007 as FUNDEB (Fundo de Manutenção e Desenvolvimento da Educação Básica e de Valorização dos Profissionais da Educação). FUNDEB extended the equalization scheme to cover pre-primary education (crèche services for children from infancy through age three and preschool for children aged four through six), as well as secondary education (grades 9–11). FUNDEB also explicitly guaranteed minimum levels of per capita funding for enrollment in education programs for indigenous and quilombo communities, and youth and adult education. The minimum funding levels per student for the different levels of education are shown in table 3.

By raising minimum spending levels in basic education, FUNDEF and FUNDEB have driven a significant increase in overall education spending in Brazil since 1998, both in real terms and as a share of GDP. From approximately 2 percent of GDP in 1995, basic education spending rose to 4 percent of GDP in 2008. If higher education is included, Brazil invested more than 5.2 percent of GDP in education in 2008, and this share continues to rise. Later in this report, we compare the level and allocation of Brazilian education spending with trends in other middle-income and OECD countries. The FUNDEF/FUNDEB reforms have transformed Brazilian education by stimulating an overall increase in basic education spending after 1998 and by improving the equity of spending across regions and jurisdictions (figure 2).

Table 3. FUNDEB-Mandated 2010 Spending Levels (2010 Rs)

	Rs/student
Early childhood development	
Crèches	1,558
Preschool	1,770
Primary education	1,416
Secondary education	1,840
Adult and youth education	1,132

Source: INEP/MEC.

Figure 2. FUNDEF/FUNDEB Expenditures, 1998-2010

(in billions of constant 2010 Rs)

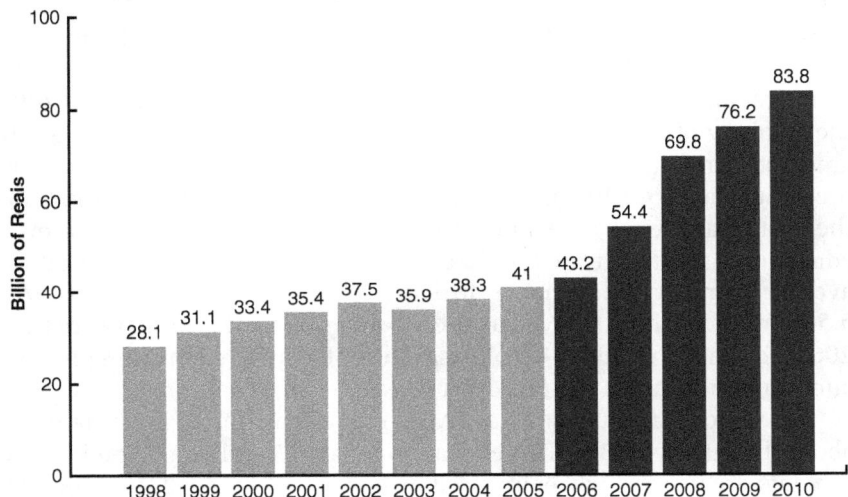

Source: National Treasury (2010).

Measuring Results

From a starting point of no information on student learning in 1994, the Cardoso and Lula da Silva administrations have systematically constructed one of the world's most impressive systems for measuring education results. In many respects, the Prova Brasil/Provinha Brasil student assessments and the IDEB (Índice de Desenvolvimento da Educação Básica) composite index of education quality developed by the Ministry of Education's assessment arm (INEP, Instituto Nacional de Estudos e Pesquisas Educacionais Anísio Teixeira) is superior to current practice in the United States and in many other OECD countries in the quantity, relevance, and quality of the student and school performance information it provides. The SAEB/Prova Brasil test and IDEB rankings have become a high-visibility source of public information on school and system performance. Equally important, they are the measurement anchor for a new wave of policies in Brazil aimed at creating stronger incentives for teachers and schools. Box 1 describes the innovative character of the IDEB tool.

Brazil initiated a technically well-designed, sample-based student assessment system (SAEB) in 1995. SAEB administered biannual tests in math and Portuguese to a nationally representative sample of students in the fourth and eighth grades of primary school and the third year of secondary school. SAEB was designed to provide representative results at the state (but not municipal) level and to permit standardized tracking of learning progress over time. In 2000, Brazil joined the OECD's Program for International Student Assessment (PISA) and worked to ensure comparability between the national and international scales. In 2005, the Ministry of Education expanded SAEB to test all fourth- and eighth-grade students in math and Portuguese every two years, and renamed the exam the Prova Brazil. (SAEB remains a sample-based assessment at the 11th-grade level.) The move to census-based application for primary education meant that for the first time, data would be available on the average learning performance in each school administered by Brazil's 5,564 municipalities (as well as the 26 states and the federal district). In 2007, the ministry added a voluntary test of third-grade reading literacy and numeracy, called the Provinha Brasil.

We will look in detail at what SAEB, Prova Brasil, and PISA data reveal about the quality of Brazilian education today. We will also examine how test data are increasingly being used by policy makers at all levels to track progress, create positive incentives, and target supplementary support for schools. The creation of the instruments and technical capacity for periodic, standardized measurement of student learning outcomes across almost 40 million students in 175,000 primary and secondary schools is a major achievement of Brazilian education officials over the past 15 years.

Reducing Schooling Costs for Poor Children

The third key education policy developed and sustained over the past two governments is a program of cash support to low-income families to protect the schooling attainment of their children. The Bolsa Escola program makes a monthly payment to families in the lowest income quintile; it was launched under the Cardoso administration in 2001 and was based on the same concept as other conditional cash transfer (CCT) programs in Latin America, such as Mexico's Progresa/Oportunidades program—that public transfers to enable poor households to invest adequately in the schooling and health of their children are crucial to break the intergenerational poverty cycle. By developing innovative distribution channels, such as ATM cards for low-income mothers who had never had a bank account before, Bolsa Escola broke new ground in terms of program administration and female empowerment.

In 2003, the Lula da Silva administration renamed the program Bolsa Família and scaled it up further by folding several other cash and in-kind

BOX 1

Avoiding Perverse Incentives: Brazil's Index of Basic Education Quality

In 2007, the Brazilian Ministry of Education introduced the Indice de Desenvolvimento da Educação Básica (IDEB), an innovative tool for systematic monitoring of basic educational progress in every school, municipality, state (and federal district), and region of the country. The innovation lies in the IDEB's combined measure of student learning results and student flows (grade progression, repetition, and graduation rates). Because the index is the product of both test scores and pass rates, it discourages schools from automatic promotion of children who are not learning. However, it also discourages schools from holding children back to boost learning scores. Avoiding incentives for grade retention is important in Brazil, where average repetition rates in primary school are approximately 20 percent, the highest in Latin America.

The IDEB builds on the progress Brazil has made in scaling up its national student assessment system to a technically well-regarded learning assessment in math and Portuguese, the Prova Brasil, that is applied every two years to all fourth- and eighth-grade students. The IDEB measure combines Prova Brasil test results with administrative data on school enrollment, repetition, and promotion. The raw scale of the exams ranges from zero to 500, and the standardized scale ranges from zero to 10. Pass rates are calculated based on the information reported by each school to the national school census taken annually by the Ministry of Education.

The IDEB index for each grade-subject is calculated as the product of the standardized Prova Brasil score for the last grade in the cycle and the average pass rate for the cycle evaluated:

$$IDEB_{asj} = ProvaBrasil_{asj} * passrate_{asj}$$

where a is the subject evaluated (Portuguese or mathematics); s is the cycle evaluated; and j is the school. The average pass rate in the cycle varies from zero to 1 (it is 1 if the pass rate equals 100 percent). The standardized IDEB measure thus varies between zero and 10.

The IDEB has been rapidly accepted in Brazil as the leading metric for gauging the relative performance of both individual schools and municipal and state systems. Biannual IDEB results are widely reported in the media, and the federal government has established targets for improvement of primary and secondary education results for every one of Brazil's 26 states (and federal district) and 5,564 municipal school systems. Within states and municipalities, the IDEB reveals the relative

(continued on next page)

> **BOX 1** *continued*
>
> performance of different schools. At the secondary school level, the index is based on the results of the SAEB student assessment (which is applied in a representative sample of schools in each state and the federal district) and student flow data. Thus, it generates state-level but not school- or municipal-level scores.
>
> One example of the IDEB's impact is the way it has facilitated the implementation of teacher bonus programs at both the state and municipal levels over the past three years. Although the different state and municipal programs in operation have various design features, all are based on annual targets for improvement in IDEB metrics. From the standpoint of federal education policy, this has created a powerful platform for comparative analysis of state (and federal district) and municipal innovations in basic education.
>
> ***Sources:*** Fernandes (2007); Fernandes and Gremaud (2009).

transfer programs into a unified targeting system with a streamlined administration. By 2009, Bolsa Família covered more than 12 million families across the country— 97.3 percent of the target population[5] (table 4). Unlike Mexico's Progresa/Oportunidades CCT, neither Bolsa Escola nor Bolsa Família was phased in using a control group to permit a rigorous evaluation of the impacts. However, a number of evaluations relying on less robust methods have found some evidence of positive effects on a range of educational outcomes, including enrollment, attendance, grade progression, retention rates, and even study time of students from beneficiary families.[6]

---

5   Ministry of Social Development, www.mds.gov.br/gestaodainformacao/mdsemnumeros.
6   For positive effects on attendance, retention, and study time, see de Oliveira (2009). For effects on attendance, grade progression, and retention, see Glewwe and Kassouf (2008).

Table 4. Expansion of Bolsa Escola/Bolsa Família, 2002-2009

	2002	2007	2009
Number of families benefitting	4.9 million[7]	11 million	12 million
Primary and secondary students benefitting	8.2 million	15.3 million	17.7 million
Amount transferred (in constant 2009 Rs)	3.4 billion	9.9 billion	11.9 billion

Sources: Ministério do Desenvolvimento Social e Combate à fome (MDS): Secretaria Nacional de Renda e de Cidadania (SENARC), and; Instituto Brasileiro de Geografia e Estatística(IBGE).

Federal Oversight

After 1995, the federal government began to play a stronger and more effective role in several areas that are key to managing a large and decentralized education system. In basic education, the government set a legal framework for the sector, established national curriculum guidelines, developed nationally vetted lists of textbooks and reading books, supported the development and delivery of teacher training and upgrading programs, and provided targeted technical and financial assistance to low-performing municipal education systems through the 2008 joint action plan, Plano de Ações Articuladas (PAR). In 2009, the government also expanded compulsory primary education from eight to nine years. Under the reform, the two-year preschool cycle begins at age 4, the nine-year primary school cycle begins at age 6 (instead of 7), and three years of secondary school begin at age 13. This makes the compulsory schooling cycle in Brazil one of the longest in the region. At the secondary level, the Lula da Silva government has also invested substantially in expanding the network of high-quality federal technical institutes (CEFETs, Centros Federais de Educação Tecnológica).

Although this report is focused on basic education, there have been advances in higher education policy as well. The ProUni program is a notable example. The program was designed to expand higher education access by subsidizing private university tuition for high-performing students from low-income families; since it was launched in 2004, more than 120,000 students a year have benefitted. The higher education participation rate of poor students remains very low, but ProUni is helping to move it in a positive direction. In other important areas, the Lula da Silva government continued the innovative Cardoso initiatives

---
7 An additional 1 million families with children from infants through six-year-olds were subsidized under the Bolsa Alimentação program.

to measure secondary school quality through a unified secondary school exit exam, ENEM (Exame Nacional de Ensino Médio) and to benchmark the relative quality of higher education programs through exit exams for key disciplines applied to university graduates across the country (ENADE, Exame Nacional de Desempenho de Estudantes). The Lula da Silva administration also increased funding for scientific research allocated through a competitive peer review mechanism and moved toward increased institutional autonomy and accountability for results in public universities.

Nonetheless, higher education policy is likely to be a key challenge for the current administration. By global standards, the share of youth enrolled in tertiary education remains extremely low, and public spending per higher education student is exceedingly high. More than 80 percent of tertiary enrollments are in private institutions that are considered of low academic quality. The high quality of the best public universities—which are the leaders in the LAC region and outrank many European universities in publications and research citations—is a justifiable source of pride. But internal efficiency, whether measured as the number of students per teacher (which is about half of the OECD ratio) or the average years it takes to complete a four-year program, is low.

Conclusion

The education landscape is changing in Brazil. Profound federal reforms of the basic education system over the past 16 years have put in place the institutional framework for a higher performing basic education system. An impressive number of governors and mayors have made education reform a political priority. Dynamic secretaries of education are moving ahead with creative programs and bold reforms that were unthinkable two decades ago. Education policy makers are beginning to support rigorous impact evaluations to determine which programs really work. Leading examples of promising reforms and evidence of their impact are highlighted throughout this report. In the next section, we assess the performance of the Brazilian education system in a global context. In the subsequent section, we analyze in greater depth the areas in which more progress is needed and review the research from Brazil and elsewhere on policies and programs that can spur improvement.

Table 5. Brazilian Basic Education 2009 - Key Statistics

Level	Number of Schools	Number of Students	Number of Teachers	Years of Cycle	Starting Age
Primary (Ensino Fundamental)	152,251	31.5 million	1,377,483	9	6
Municipal	104,494	17.3 million			
Schools with fewer than 30 students	42,585	.7 million			
Private schools	20,297	3.7 million			
Secondary (Ensino Médio)	25,923	8.3 million	461,542	3	14
Federal technical schools	217	.09 million			
Private schools	7,415	.97 million			
Pre-primary (not including daycare) (Pré-escola)	114,158	6.7 million	369,698	2	4
Private	27,799	1.8 million			
Other (e.g., adult ed., etc.) (Educação de Jovens e Adultos, Educação Especial)		5.7 million			
TOTAL	197,468	53.8 million	1,977,978		

Source: INEP, Censo Escolar (2009).

Note: (1) The total number of school establishments is smaller than the sum of primary and secondary schools because preschools, primary, schools, and secondary schools can share buildings. Similarly, the total number of teachers is smaller than the sum of teachers by level because some teachers work in multiple assignments. (2) The 2009 data reflect the extension of the primary school cycle from eight to nine years of schooling, beginning at age six. The implementation of this change in 2009 creates a break in enrollment data for both preschool (previously ages four through six, now ages three through five) and primary school in comparison with enrollment data for previous years.

2

Brazilian Basic Education: Meeting the Challenge?

Education systems play a critical role in every country in empowering people to develop their full human capabilities, building national unity, transmitting national culture, and stimulating social development. But from an economic standpoint, an education system is judged by how efficiently it performs three paramount functions: (1) developing the labor force skills required for sustained economic growth; (2) contributing to the reduction of poverty and inequality by providing educational opportunity for all; and (3) transforming education spending into educational results—above all, student learning. How does Brazil compare with other countries in meeting these challenges?

Meeting the Needs of a 21st Century Economy

Brazil's integration into the world economy is projected to increase significantly in the coming decade. With a trade-to-GDP ratio of 20 percent, it is still one of the least open economies in the world; among OECD countries, for example, only Japan and the United States have lower traded shares in total output. Greater economic integration offers the promise of higher and more sustainable economic growth, but it also means increasing pressure on the Brazilian labor force to reach globally competitive levels of productivity. Many factors affect labor productivity, export competitiveness, and attractiveness to global investment, but research has consistently pointed to human capital accumulation as a critical element. Traditionally, a nation's human capital has been measured as the average years of schooling of the labor force—which has grown faster in Brazil since 1990 than in any other major country.

Learning Is What Counts for Growth

Over the past decade, education researchers have shown that what counts for economic growth is what students actually learn, and not how many years of schooling they complete. Moreover, the crucial yardstick is not national standards but the best performing education systems globally. Analyzing data on student performance on internationally benchmarked tests—such as the Program for International Assessment (PISA), the Trends in International Mathematics and Science Study (TIMSS), and the Program on International Reading Literacy Study (PIRLS)—from more than 50 countries over a 40-year period, Hanushek and Woessmann (2007) have demonstrated a tight correlation between average student learning levels and long-term economic growth. A country with average test performance one standard deviation higher than another's (approximately the difference between the average scores of Brazil and the United Kingdom or Norway) on the 2009 PISA will have enjoyed a 2 percentage point higher average annual growth rate of GDP over the 1960–2000 period.

As shown in figures 3 and 4, the relationship holds across high-income countries, low-income countries, and regions: differences in average cognitive skills are consistently and highly correlated with long-term rates of per capita income growth. Moreover, while the *quantity of education* (average years of schooling of the labor force) is statistically significantly related to long-term economic growth in analyses that neglect education quality, the association between years of schooling and growth falls to close to zero once *education quality* (measured by average scores on internationally benchmarked tests) is introduced. It is the quality of education that counts for economic benefits from schooling.

Brazil's consistent participation in the OECD's PISA since 2000 has generated excellent comparative data on how its average student learning stacks up. PISA 2009 results confirm the country's significant, sustained progress. In mathematics, Brazil ranked second to last among participating countries in 2000 (only Peru was lower). By 2009, Brazil's 52-point increase in math was one of the largest on record.[8] Brazil's average score across the three disciplines tested (reading, math, and science) rose 33

---

8   The PISA secretariat reports math trends using 2003 as the base year, due to changes in the test instrument between 2000 and 2003. However, an analysis of the math test sections that are comparable from 2000-2003 confirms that Brazil's improvement over this period was equally strong.

Chapter 2: Brazilian Basic Education: Meeting the Challenge? | 17

Figure 3. Cognitive Skills and Economic Growth Across Regions

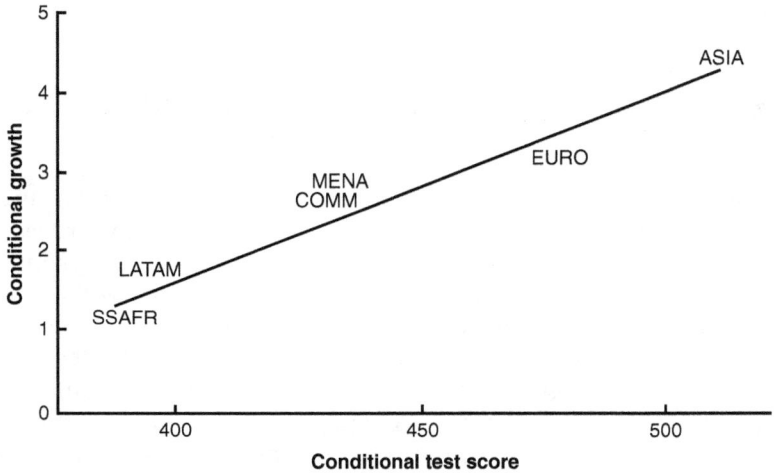

Added-variable plot of a regression of the average annual rate of growth (in percent) of real GDP per capita in 1960–2000 on the initial level of real GDP per capita in 1960 and average scores on international student achievement tests (mean of the unconditional variables added to each axis). Based on Table 2, column (1). See Table 1 for a list of countries contained in each world region. Region codes: Asia (ASIA), Commonwealth OECD members (COMM), Europe (EURO), Latin America (LATAM), Middle East and North Africa (MENA), Sub-Saharan Africa (SSAFR).

Sources: Hanushek and Woessmann (2007).

Figure 4. Cognitive Skills and Economic Growth Across Countries

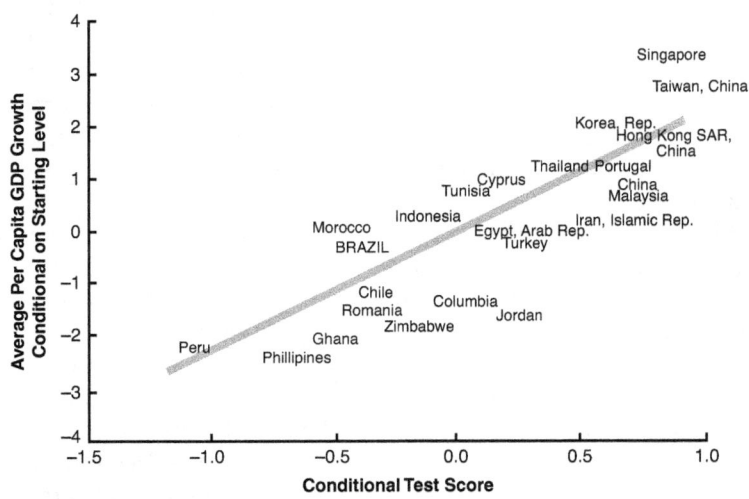

Sources: Hanushek and Woessmann (2007).

points over the decade, from 368 to 401. This represents the third largest improvement of any country over the period, after Luxembourg (38-point increase) and Chile (37-point increase).

Brazilian Skills Are Improving but Still Lag Those of Other Countries

Despite the impressive progress, Brazil is still far from achieving the average learning levels, secondary education completion rates, and student flow efficiency of the OECD and other middle-income countries. As shown in figure 5, Brazil's learning outcomes are below the average for middle-income countries and even below those of some lower income countries, such as Thailand and Jordan. Nor is Brazil a leader in Latin America: Chile, Uruguay, and Mexico all perform better in absolute terms. And while LAC countries as a group substantially trail the OECD average performance, the first-time entry of another BRIC (Brazil, Russia, India, China) member into PISA (Shanghai, China) set an even higher benchmark (figure 6). The approximately 210-point gap in math skills between the average student in Shanghai and the average Brazilian student is equivalent to approximately five school years.

Analysis also reveals that the main reason for Brazil's improvement has not been an increase in the average math proficiency levels of Brazilian ninth graders—which have stayed relatively flat—but a reduction in age-grade distortion among the population of 15-year-olds tested. In 2000, 43 percent of the Brazilian sample had not yet reached the expected grade (ninth); by 2009, this share had declined to 25 percent. This is an important improvement, as Brazil's extraordinarily high repetition rates and age-grade distortion are serious efficiency issues. But the PISA results through 2009 do not show Brazilian ninth graders closing the gap with OECD learning levels; they mainly show more students getting to the appropriate grade on time.

The PISA test is constructed to measure trends in countries' average student scores over time relative to the mean score of 500 achieved by the OECD countries as a group in the year 2000, and to measure the percentage of students in each country scoring above a high performance threshold (proficiency level 5 or 6, roughly equivalent to a score of 600 or more) and a low performance threshold of level 1 (roughly equivalent to a score of 400). Students scoring at this level or below are considered to lack even the most basic literacy and numeracy skills. Decomposition of Brazil's 2009 performance shows that, despite the country's progress in math, 60 percent of students still scored below 400 (i.e., they lacked a minimum set of numeracy skills). Across the OECD, only 14 percent of

Chapter 2: Brazilian Basic Education: Meeting the Challenge? | 19

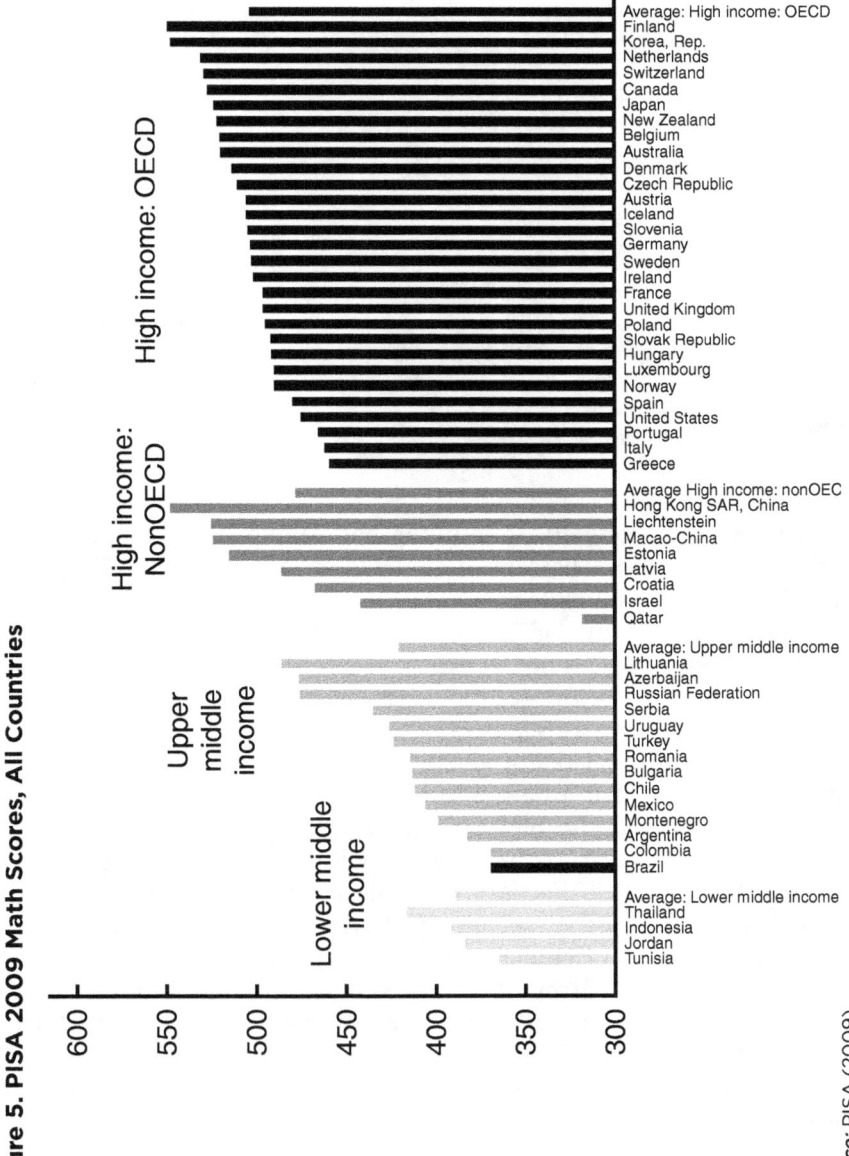

Figure 5. PISA 2009 Math Scores, All Countries

Source: PISA (2009).

Figure 6. Brazil's PISA Math Performance, 2000–2009

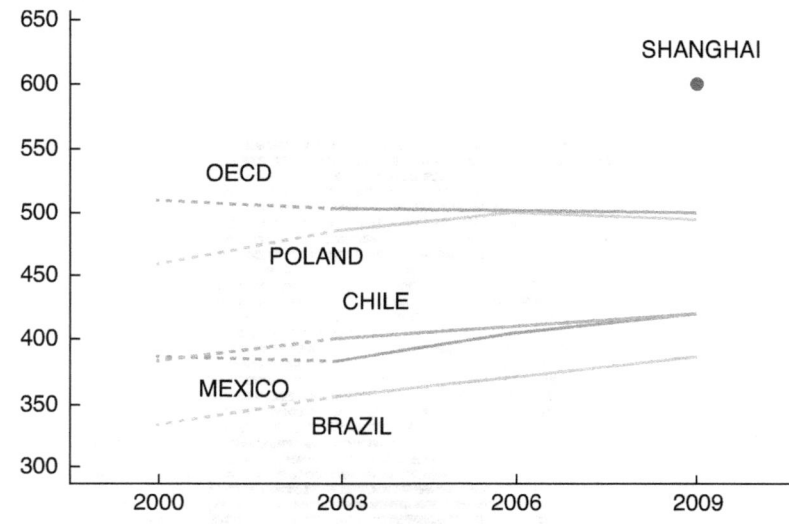

Source: OECD (2010).

students scored below 400, and in top-performing Korea and Shanghai, only 5 percent and 3 percent of students, respectively, did. Comparing the distribution of students across these performance bands in 2009 gives a graphic sense of how far Brazilian education lags competitor countries (figure 7). Box 2 gives some examples of questions that 15 year old students who score below 400 cannot answer correctly.

Although it is easy to see how a large share of students lacking basic skills might constrain labor productivity and economic growth, Hanushek and Woessmann (2007) have also analyzed the importance of a critical mass of students at the high-performance end of the spectrum: "Is it a few rocket scientists at the very top who spur economic growth, or is it education for all that lays a broad base at the lower parts of the distribution?" When they separately analyze the cross-country learning data for the share of students above each threshold, both the broad diffusion of basic literacy skills across the population and having a significant share of top performers seem to exert separately identifiable effects on economic growth.

Here, Brazil's performance is equally troubling. Whereas 53 percent of 15-year-olds in Shanghai, 28 percent in Korea, and 15 percent across all OECD countries have high-level math skills (scoring over 600), only 1 percent of Brazilian students perform at this level.

BOX 2

Basic Numeracy as Measured on PISA

On the 2006 PISA, students who could not answer math questions at the lowest level of difficulty (level 1) scored roughly 400, on average. Level 1 questions are presented in a familiar context, are clearly defined, and require very limited math skills—only the ability to understand simple texts and link explicit information to a basic mathematical calculation.

The two questions below correspond to level 1. In 2006, 80 percent of students in OECD countries answered these questions correctly, while only 11 percent of Brazilian students could do so.

Question 1. Speed of a Racing Car
This graph shows how the speed of a racing car varies along a flat 3 kilometer track during its second lap.

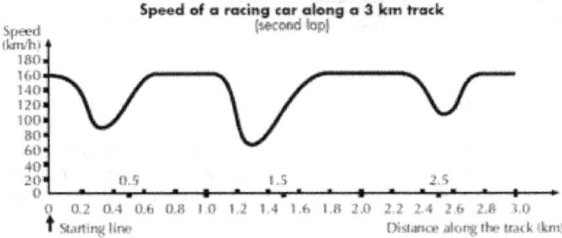

Where was the lowest speed recorded during the second lap?
A. at the starting line.
B. at about 0.8 km.
C. at about 1.3 km. (correct answer)
D. halfway around the track.

Question 2. Exchange Rate
Mei-Ling from Singapore was preparing to go to South Africa for 3 months as an exchange student. She needed to change some Singapore dollars (SGD) into South African rand (ZAR). Mei-Ling found out that the exchange rate between Singapore dollars and South African rand was 1 SGD = 4.2 ZAR. Mei-Ling changed 3,000 Singapore dollars into South African rand at this exchange rate. How much money in South African rand did Mei-Ling get?
Correct answer: 12,600 ZAR

Sources: PISA 2006 - Science Competencies for Tomorrow's World, Vol. 1 (Ch. 6: A Profile of Student Performance in Reading and Mathematics from PISA 2000 to PISA 2006) and Take the Test: Sample Questions from OECD's PISA Assessments 2000–2006.

Contributed by Debora Brakarz

Figure 7. Comparative PISA Math Proficiency, 2009

(percentage of students scoring at high, average, and below basic levels)

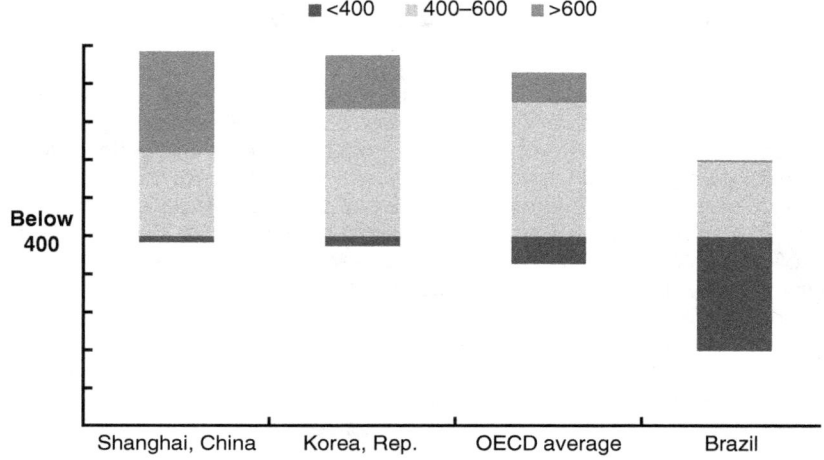

Source: PISA database (2009).

Note: Bars are anchored to the "below 400" threshold. Percentages for the three groups add up to 100 percent. Thresholds map to PISA standardized scores. A score of 500 represents the mean score, and 100 points is the score associated with 1 standard deviation.

The PISA tests only secondary school (ninth-grade) students, but Brazil's excellent national testing system—SAEB and Prova Brasil—tracks learning levels of students in 4th, 8th, and 11th grade. The Provinha Brasil test introduced in 2007 tracks learning of third graders. Figure 8 shows the most important national trends. First, we can see a clear decline in average learning levels from 1997 to 2000. This is expected, as the rapid expansion of schooling access, primary completion, and secondary participation rates over this period drew a large number of poor and academically unprepared children into the school system. Second, considering this context, there was a modest but encouraging uptick in learning outcomes from 2001 to 2003, which was also reflected in PISA. Third, progress clearly slowed after 2003, but it appears to have resumed since 2005: Brazil's 2009 PISA performance reflected an upward trend.

Following Hanushek and Woessmann's evidence that the evolution of the top and bottom ends of the performance distribution were both important for long-term growth, we decomposed Brazilian reading and math scores on PISA by performance band to analyze the trends over time (Figure 9). They are quite different. Brazil's performance in reading

Figure 8. Math Proficiency on SAEB/Prova Brasil, 1995-2009

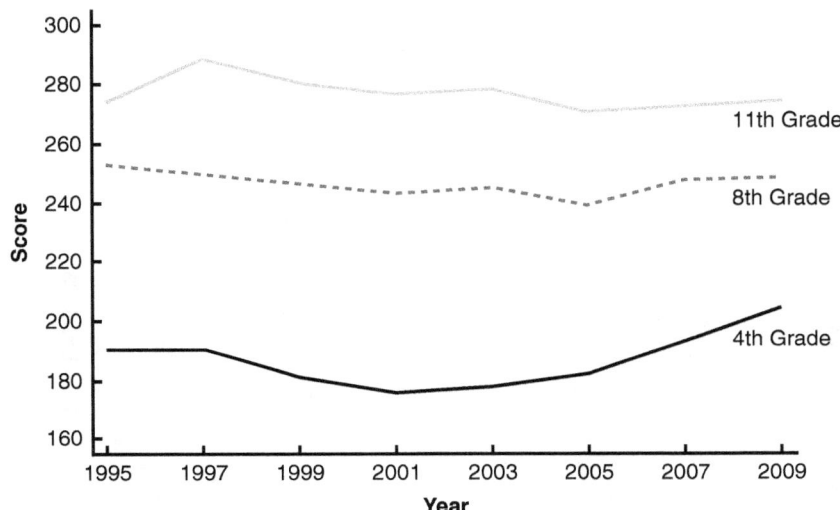

Source: National System for Evaluation of Basic Education (SAEB) (1995-2005); SAEB/Prova Brasil (2007-2009).

Note: Public schools only. For 4th and 8th grades, state and municipal schools. For 11th grade, state schools.

shows no clear trend. The share of students at the very lowest levels of performance (level 1 and below) showed no improvement from 2000 through 2006, then improved slightly in 2009. The share of students that lacked basic literacy skills in 2009 remained about the same as it was in 2003: 50 percent of test takers. This is not encouraging. At the high end of the scale, the share of students performing at level 5 or 6 also fluctuated over the period, but in 2009 it was still a tiny 1.3 percent of test takers. Equally troubling is the apparent lack of progress in bringing the lowest performing students up to a basic level of literacy by global standards.

In math, there has been clear progress in raising the skills of the very lowest performing students. The share of students scoring below level 1 dropped from 53 percent in 2003 (the first year comparable disaggregated data are available) to 38 percent in 2009—a substantial move in the right direction. However, considering that level 1 represents inadequate mastery of basic math skills, the picture is not encouraging. While the share of students performing at and below level 1 is shrinking, it remains high. And it appears that most of the improvement in Brazil's average math scores over

Figure 9. Share of Brazilian Students by Proficiency Level, Reading and Math, PISA 2000–2009

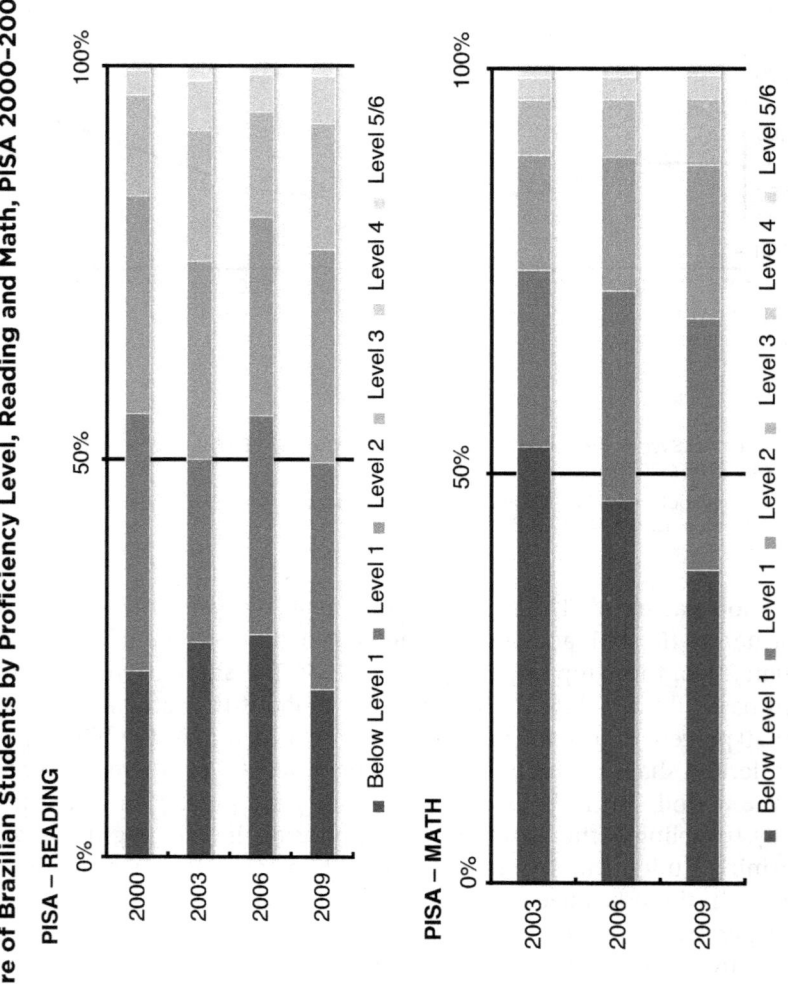

Source: PISA database (2000–2009).

the decade was driven by progress at the low end—the share of students at the highest performance levels in math did not increase.

In light of the educational performance of middle-income competitor countries, especially in East Asia but also in Latin America, it is hard to overstate the urgency of faster improvement in learning achievement at the high end in Brazil.

Economic Returns

The massive expansion of schooling in Brazil over the past 15 years has had dramatic effects on the educational structure of the labor force. In 1993, close to 70 percent of the working population aged 26–30 had less than 11 years of schooling; today that number is 40 percent. Figure 10 shows how the educational attainment curve has shifted upward over the past 15 years. The biggest change is not in initial access to primary school; even in 1993, virtually all children started school. The change has been in the number of children who stay in school through secondary education. The share of children who complete primary education has increased from roughly 42 percent to 71 percent, and the share of children who complete secondary school has risen from 28 percent to 55 percent. Access to tertiary education remains low.

Table 6 presents data on changes in real wages by years of schooling over the period, while figure 11 shows these trends graphically. Given the huge increase in the share of workers with secondary education, it is not surprising that the real wage for those workers fell by almost 10 percent. It increased until 1998, declined sharply through 2003, and has rebounded somewhat, although it still reflects no premium in the labor market for completing secondary school. There has also been significant volatility in real wages for workers with tertiary education, but the change over the period is positive, with an increase of 8.4 percent. Wages for primary school graduates have increased modestly. Finally, there has been a very large increase in the real wage for workers with four or fewer years of schooling.

Several factors explain these somewhat unusual patterns. The stagnation in the returns to secondary education over the period as a whole is consistent with the possibility that the huge increase in supply outstripped the growth of labor market demand for this level of skills. The sharp decline in real salaries through 2003 could also be explained by the SAEB evidence that average skill levels declined over this period of massive expansion in secondary enrollment. The rise in real wages for secondary graduates between 2003 and 2009 could be consistent with Brazil's PISA results, which show improvement in average skill levels of

Figure 10. Change in Average Educational Attainment in Brazil, 1993-2009

(percentage of the population aged 26-30)

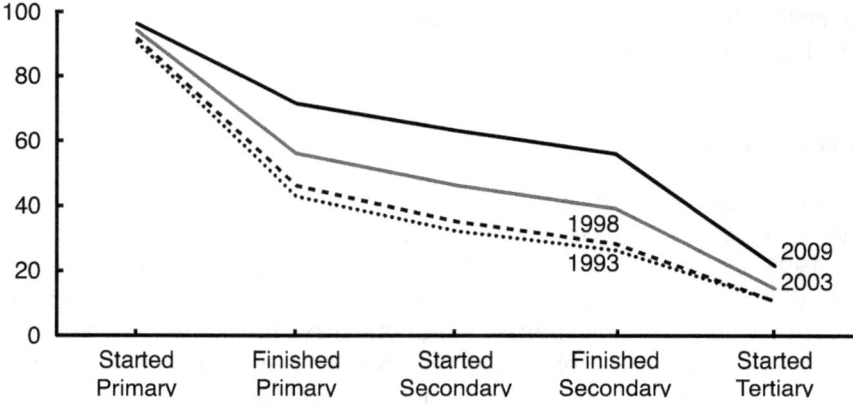

Source: PNAD, various years.

Table 6. Average Real Wages by Years of Schooling, 1993-2009

(2009 Constant Rs)

Schooling (grades completed)	1993	1998	2003	2009	Change 1993–2009
4 years	445	518	411	513	15.3%
8 years	659	779	750	714	8.4%
11 years	926	1049	750	856	-7.5%
12 or more years	1590	2011	1590	1774	11.6%

Source: PNAD.

secondary-level students, particularly in math. But it is hard to determine how much these patterns were affected by supply-side factors and how much by demand-side factors, such as the growth of industries and occupations that require secondary graduates.

The increase in real wages for the shrinking number of persons with very low levels of education is a very unusual phenomenon. Economists such as Paes de Barros attribute it to the impact of minimum wage laws and nonincome transfers, as well as more integration between urban and rural labor markets, which boosts the demand for relatively unskilled labor (Paes de Barros et al. 2010).

Figure 11. Shifts in Real Wages for Workers by Years of Schooling, 1993-2009

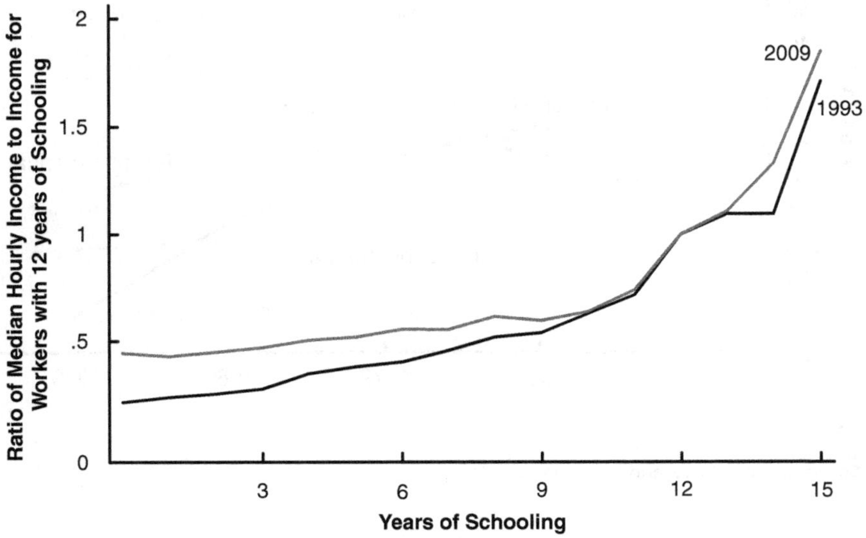

[Chart: Ratio of Median Hourly Income to Income for Workers with 12 years of Schooling vs. Years of Schooling, showing curves for 1993 and 2009]

Source: PNAD.
Note: For workers aged 26-30.

Future Trends

Hanushek and Woessmann's (2007) evidence that cognitive skill levels of workers are strongly correlated with a country's economic growth is consistent with recent research on long-term trends in the U.S. labor market demand for workers with strong analytical skills. In an influential study, Autor, Levy, and Murnane (2003) traced the increasing importance of nonroutine (higher order) tasks in the job content of major occupational categories in the U.S. economy and the declining importance of routine tasks (see figure 12). Their research showed that many cognitive tasks that used to be performed by workers with modest levels of education are now performed by computers, while many manual tasks with little skill requirement have been moved to offshore production. At the same time, the data suggest that computers complement the performance of more educated workers in complex tasks, increasing their productivity. There is also an observable trend toward more complex (often team-based) activities that create labor demand for higher level communication and interpersonal skills. The evolution in the demand for different skills in

Figure 12. Changing Demand for Skills in the U.S. Economy, 1959–1999

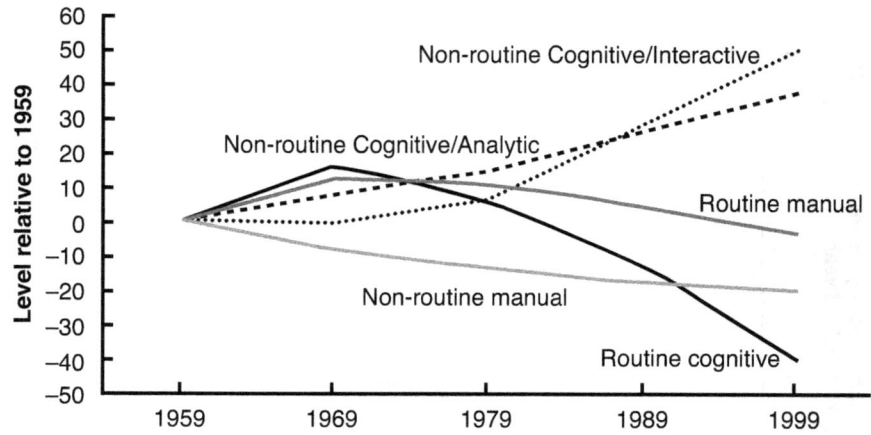

Sources: Autor, Levy, and Murnane (2003).

the labor market is reflected in the market returns to those skills. This evolution has been labeled "skill-biased technological change."

We examined Brazilian occupational data for evidence of similar trends. As figure 13 shows, the structure of the labor force has clearly shifted in Brazil over the past decade. The share of workers in blue collar jobs has declined from about 60 percent to 50 percent, and professional/managerial and other white collar jobs have increased.

However, the "new economy" skill structure in Brazil is far less pronounced than it is in the United States. We carried out a parallel analysis, following the skill groupings defined by Autor and colleagues, to determine how quickly the demand for higher order analytical and interpersonal skills was growing in Brazil.[9] The shifts in the U.S. economy observed by Autor and colleagues occurred over a period of 40 years, although they accelerated over the past 20 years, no doubt as a result of the spread of personal computing and the internet. These factors might be expected to affect developing country economies more rapidly as they absorb current technologies.

We synthesized our findings by comparing a simplified version of figure 12 for the U.S. economy over the 1981–2009 period with a parallel figure for Brazil. In figure 14, we combined the nonroutine or high-level analytical, interpersonal, and manual skills that Autor and colleagues

---

9   Annex 5 describes our methodology for mapping skills to occupational tasks using Brazilian labor market data.

Figure 13. Changes in Brazil's Occupational Structure, 1980-2009

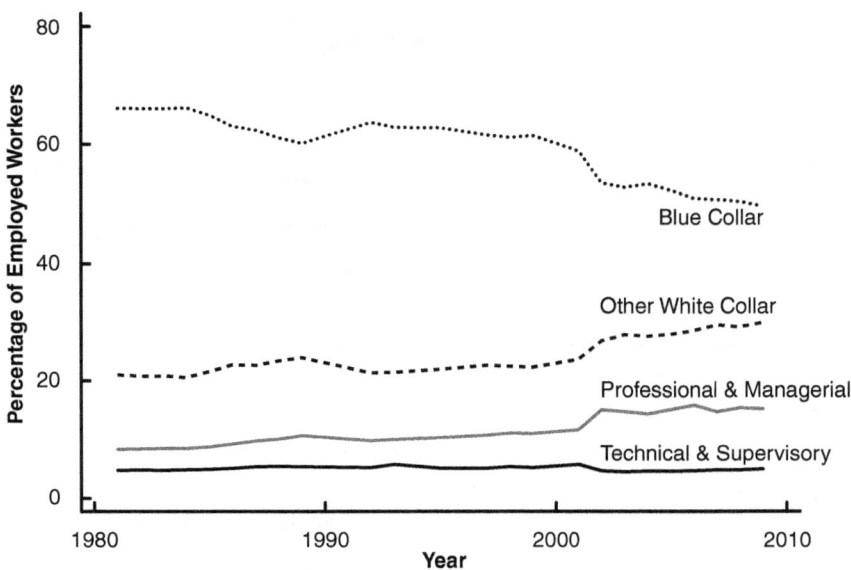

Source: PNAD (2009).

Note: Occupational codes for each decade were mapped to the corresponding code in the ISCO-88 classification scheme, then these codes were aggregated into the five categories shown in the graph.

called "new economy skills" (college-educated professionals, lawyers, doctors, and finance and business executives) into a single variable and compared this with "routine cognitive skills" (bookkeepers, accountants, audit clerks, cashiers, telephone operators) and routine manual skills (construction workers, machine operators, cooks, agricultural labor).

Not surprisingly, the analysis shows that the Brazilian labor force has not experienced the large expansion of jobs demanding new economy skills seen in the U.S. economy over the past 20 years. Both economies show a relative decline in the share of the labor force employed in jobs involving manual skills. The striking difference is that while routine cognitive skills have declined in importance in the U.S. economy – reflecting computerization and offshoring—their role in the Brazilian labor market has increased. This appears broadly consistent with the growth of "other white collar" occupations in Brazil shown in figure 13. The important observation for Brazilian education policy is that changes in job content are moving in the new economy skill direction, although at a low speed.

Figure 14. Evolution of Skills in the Labor Force: United States and Brazil, 1981–2009

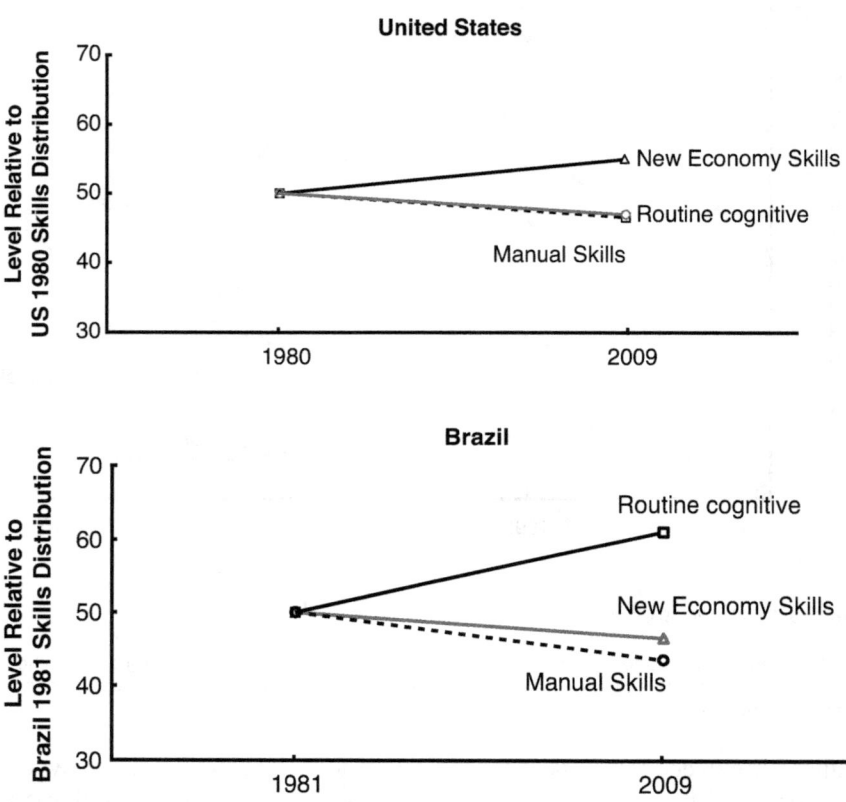

Source: Authors' estimates, from annex 5.

Note: Distributions are anchored to the 1980 (in the case of the US) and 1981 (in the case of Brazil) skills distributions of the entire labor force.

Analyzing the data by income quintile provides additional perspective. In the current Brazilian labor force, the top two income quintiles are employed in occupations that look very much like the U.S. economy (figure 15). These jobs demand the same kind of high-level analytical and interpersonal skills as the majority of occupations in the United States. Among the richest Brazilians, the importance of jobs that require routine cognitive skills or manual skills has stagnated or declined since 1981.

Obviously, not all economies will duplicate the labor market structure of the United States. Trade openness, national comparative advantage, and growth rates will influence the distribution of global economic

Figure 15. Skills Evolution in the Top Two Quintiles of the Brazilian Labor Force, 1981-2009

Note: Distribution is anchored to the 1981 skills distribution of the entire labor force.

activity, the demand for domestic factors of production, and the "race between education and technology" that plays out in every country. But available data point to rising economic returns for high-level cognitive skills in Brazil, as in the OECD countries and other middle-income countries. These 21st century skills include the ability to think analytically, manage large bodies of information and data, ask critical questions, learn new skills, and adapt to changing careers and employment across one's adult life. High-level communication and interpersonal skills—including foreign language mastery and the ability to work effectively in teams and on collaborative tasks—are also important. OECD education systems are focused on building these competencies, and these trends have major implications for the Brazilian higher education system. Many of these were laid out in the 2008 World Bank report on Knowledge and Innovation for Competitiveness (World Bank, 2008b). The overriding implication for the basic education system in Brazil is the urgent need to increase student learning.

Reducing Inequality and Poverty

Broadbased access to education not only develops the skills of the labor force; it creates the platform for a more equal society. Education systems that function well afford talented and motivated individuals from all strata of society a route to higher skills, occupations, and incomes, with the promise of upward social mobility. Brazil has historically been one of the most unequal countries in the world. On the Gini index, on which European nations and Canada score between 0.24 and 0.36 (with zero denoting perfect equality), the estimate for Brazil in 1993 was 0.52. Paes de Barros (2010) concluded that two-thirds of Brazilian wage inequality could be attributed to the unequal distribution of education.

The substantial expansion of schooling attainment in Brazil over the past 15 years would be expected to increase income equality, and it has. The 2008 Gini coefficient for Brazil was estimated at 0.45, which is a substantial change by global standards. Most researchers attribute the change primarily to progressive government policies. Cash transfers to low-income families began under the Cardoso administration with the Bolsa Escola. The Lula da Silva administration consolidated and expanded these transfers under Bolsa Família and instituted a major increase in the minimum wage and in pensions. These factors likely explain the significant rise in income in this period for people with limited schooling.

Schooling access and educational attainment have also been broadly expanded across Brazil. Figure 16 shows the significant rise in average schooling levels in all regions from 1993 through 2009. The northeast region started at a low point and continues to lag other regions in average educational attainment, although it has made strong progress.

Over the past generation, entry to primary schooling has been fairly equal across regions; educational disparity begins to occur during the course of the primary cycle. In the northeast, only 57 percent of students complete the cycle, compared with 76 percent in the southeast and south (figure 17). For students who complete primary school, the rates of transition to secondary school, persistence in secondary school, and completion of secondary school are very similar across regions. Rates of transition to tertiary education are also remarkably similar, conditional on secondary school completion, with a clear bottleneck in access to tertiary education across all regions.

An important source of disparity in educational attainment is location. At least through the 1990s, a large disparity in schooling attainment persisted between urban and rural children. It does not stem from access—even 20 years ago, close to 90 percent of children in rural areas enrolled in primary school. But only 35 percent completed the cycle, compared with 75 percent in urban areas. Among rural children who manage to complete primary school, a relatively high share continue on to secondary school, and they tend to complete secondary school at the same rate as children in urban areas. These patterns confirm a central challenge of ensuring adequate schooling quality and increasing the primary completion rate in rural areas (figure 18).

Figure 16. Regional Trends in Educational Attainment, 1993–2009

(years of schooling completed by population aged 26–30)

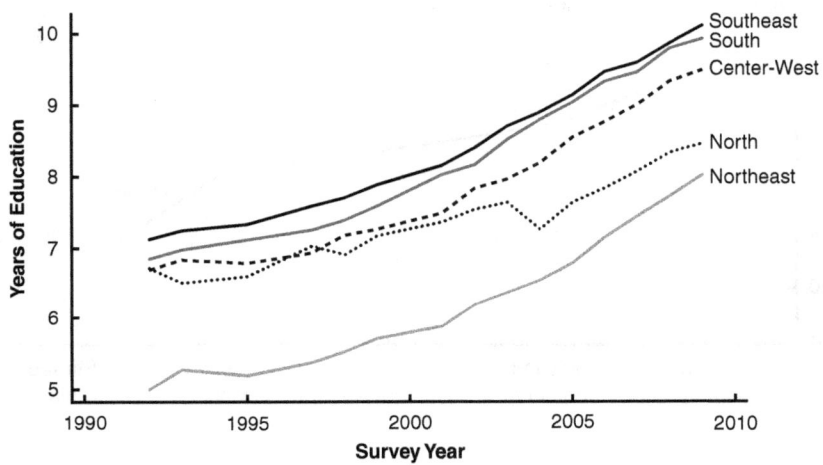

Note: PNAD, various years.

Figure 17. Educational Attainment by Region, 2009

(percentage of the population aged 26–30)

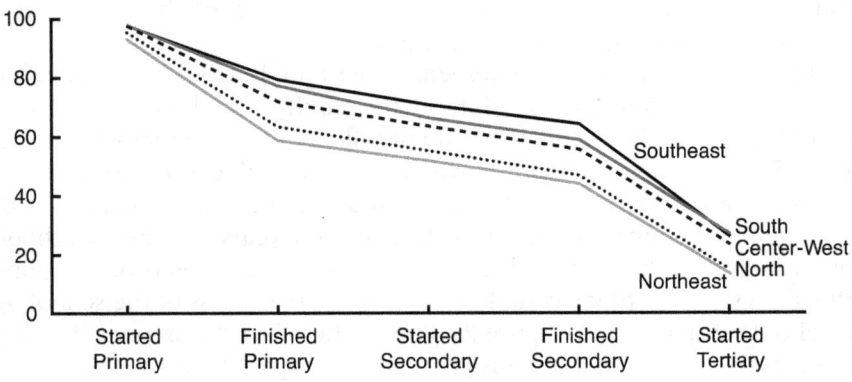

Note: PNAD (2009).

Figure 18. Educational Attainment for Urban and Rural Populations, 2009

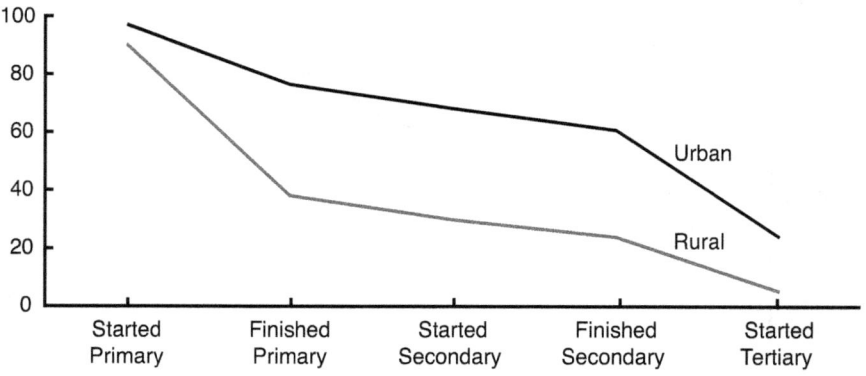

Note: PNAD (2009).

Cross-sectional data that reveal the schooling trajectory for children from different regions or households, such as in figures 17 and 18, are a look in the rearview mirror. They describe what happened to people who started school 20 years ago. There is little question that FUNDEF/FUNDEB, Bolsa Família, and state and municipal education reform efforts have improved the quality of education in most rural regions, such as the north and northeast. Some evidence for this is the improvement in fourth-grade learning outcomes in these regions over the past several years on the SAEB/Prova Brasil (figure 19).

The expansion in secondary enrollment in Brazil has produced a significant intergenerational shift in the equity of schooling. Parental education used to be a major predictor of children's educational attainment. In 1993, secondary education was largely available only to students whose parents had been educated to that level. The child of a father with no formal schooling would complete only four years of primary school, on average. This has changed dramatically: the median years of schooling Brazilian students today complete is 10 or 11, regardless of the schooling level of their parents. As figure 20 shows, there is a striking equalization of schooling attainment for this generation compared with their parents, whose schooling attainment ranged from zero to ten years.

The doors to schooling are clearly open to children from all families in Brazil, and programs such as Bolsa Família have helped narrow the

Figure 19. Fourth-Grade Math Performance by Region, 1999-2009

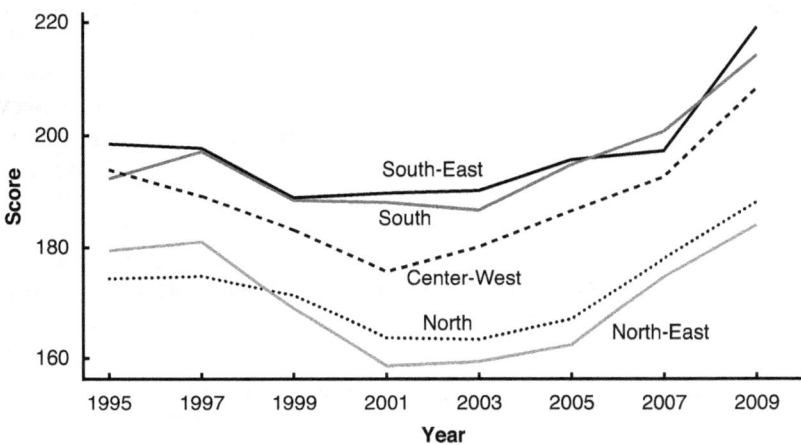

Note: 1995-2005 scores are from SAEB; 2007 and 2009 scores are from SAEB/Prova Brasil.

Figure 20. Educational Attainment of 20-Year-Olds Compared with Their Household Heads, 1993-2009

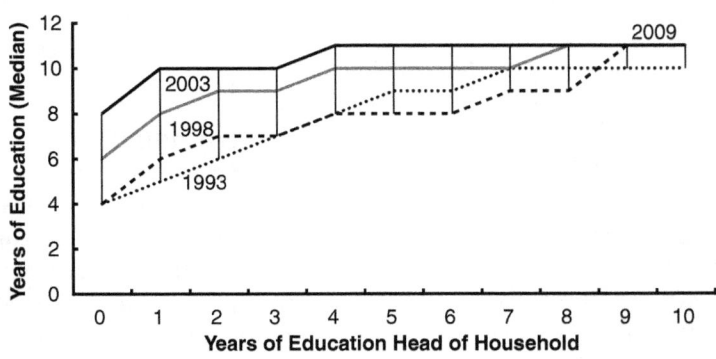

Note: PNAD, various years.

gap in educational attainment between children from the top and bottom income groups over the past decade and a half. Learning outcomes for students from the lowest income quintiles have also improved, and the rise in PISA scores for the two lowest income quintiles over the past three years is particularly impressive. Unlike some of the other Latin American countries that participated, Brazil boosted PISA scores more for the lowest income groups than for the richer quintiles (figure 21). However, household income is still the best predictor of what level of schooling a child will attain, and although the gaps in both educational attainment and learning levels between the top and bottom income quintiles have narrowed, they are far from eliminated.

Figure 21. Years of Schooling Completed and PISA Math Performance by Household Income Quintile

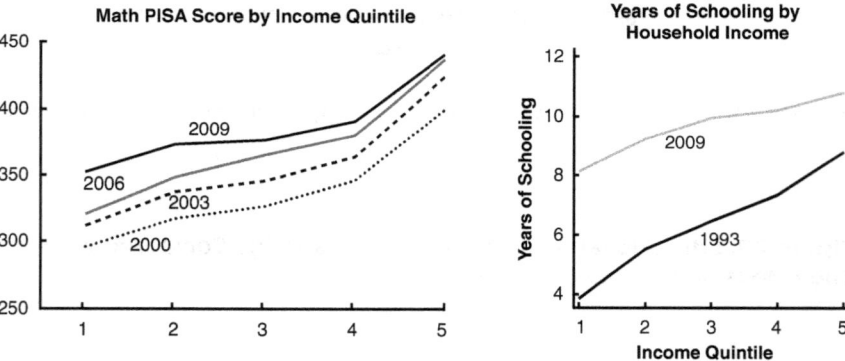

Sources: PNAD 1993 and 2009; PISA data 2000-2009.

In Brazil, as in other countries, the issues underlying the low educational attainment of children from poor families have become more complex over time. Physical access to schools and household budget constraints have receded in importance, while social issues (teen pregnancy, gang and drug involvement), family instability (unemployment, domestic violence, homelessness), and learning issues and developmental deficits stemming from children's earliest years have become more prominent. These issues affect the demand side of schooling: the willingness and ability of students to make use of the educational services they are offered.

The average quality of schooling available to low-income students in Brazil may be lower than that available to students in high-income areas. However, recent research in Brazil, the United States, and elsewhere points to large variations in teacher quality and effectiveness across different classrooms in the same school (whether in a low- or high-income neighborhood) that dwarf the variations in quality among schools. Student learning in the federal technical schools and high-fee private schools in Brazil is dramatically higher than in public systems. But when we control for student background characteristics, most of the gap disappears.

What remains apparent in Brazil is a belief among some teachers that poor children cannot learn. We discuss this issue, and how progressive education secretaries across Brazil are trying to deal with it, in the next section.

If the core equity issue in Brazilian education has shifted from equalizing access to equalizing learning attainment, what policies best address this issue? Secretaries of basic education in Brazil are increasingly focusing on two major strategies consistent with global best practice:

1. Preventive interventions—expanded early childhood development services for low-income families and at-risk children.

2. Remedial interventions—remedial tutoring, accelerated learning programs, extended school day, and other programs targeting children with special learning needs, emotional needs, or other disadvantages, to help them keep up with their peers.

Early Childhood Development: Leveling the Playing Field

Research on early childhood brain development is generating powerful evidence of the stark divergence in cognitive function that takes place in the earliest years of life between children from advantaged and disadvantaged home environments. Evidence from the United Sates, Argentina, Bolivia, and other countries shows that early childhood education (ECE) programs—especially high-quality, targeted programs—can prevent these deficits in cognitive and long-term educational performance of the poorest children.[10] With the extension of FUNDEB financing to cover crèche and ECE enrollment, municipal education secretariats across Brazil are moving rapidly to extend existing services and experiment with new models. There is a widespread recognition that the next critical social challenge in Brazil is protecting the human potential of children born into disadvantaged families.

Bolsa Família is not only an efficient program of income transfers but also an administrative mechanism for reaching and tracking the progress

---

10   For evidence from the United States, see Almond and Currie (2011); for Argentina, see Berlinski, Galiani, and Gertler (2009); for Bolivia, see Behrman, Cheng, and Todd (2004).

of poor households. Progressive municipal education secretaries are developing ways to link the program with direct actions to ensure that children in poor households have access to adequate health screening, nutrition, and cognitive and social stimulation from birth. We discuss some of the most promising approaches in the next section. Access to ECE services remains highly constrained for the lowest income groups in Brazil, but it will be crucial for long-term progress in raising the educational attainment of poor children.

Remediating Learning Gaps: Helping Kids Catch Up

Children from low-income families are by no means the only students with learning disabilities, attention deficits, and physical or emotional issues that can challenge teachers. But the poorest children are more likely to either start school behind in learning or fall behind. Brazil has an entrenched tradition of making slow learners repeat grades. In the next section, we assess this policy from an efficiency standpoint; here we focus on the equity implications.

National household survey (PNAD) data reveal that it takes children from the lowest income quintile, on average, three extra years to complete primary school. They have the lowest primary and secondary school completion rates, because the opportunity costs of remaining in school grow with each year of repetition until they are prohibitive. Brazil's high rates of grade repetition and the age-grade distortion they create have no parallel in the OECD world or elsewhere in Latin America. Only a handful of francophone African countries repeat students at Brazil's high rate.

A large amount of the program innovation going on in Brazil today—much of it supported by influential foundations—is aimed at developing effective remedial learning programs. One of the largest scale efforts is the Reforço Escolar launched by Rio de Janeiro municipality in 2009, which tests all children before the school year and provides two weeks of intensive tutoring to those who are not at grade level. In 2010, the program provided special math and reading reinforcement to more than 200,000 students.

In 1995, the state of São Paulo—in collaboration with the nonprofit foundation CENPEC (Centro de Estudos em Pesquisa Educação e Ação Comunitária)—developed an accelerated learning program (Programa de Correção de Fluxo) for the first cycle of basic education, targeted at students with high age-grade distortion (see Reali et al. 2006). The following year, the state of Paraná worked with CENPEC to expand the program into the second cycle of basic education.

The private sector has been active in supporting public school systems in this area: CENPEC now supports accelerated learning programs in 16 states and numerous municipalities. These programs group students with age-grade distortion into separate classes and provide them with a thematically focused curriculum. The Fundação Roberto Marinho has developed a number of Telecurso programs geared to helping overage students in the last three grades of primary school and in secondary school get back on grade level. These programs use one specially trained teacher, supported by sophisticated video/DVD programs, to teach an accelerated learning course across all subjects. The pedagogical approach emphasizes classroom discussion to ensure that students are engaged and internalize the material. The programs manage to condense the last three grades of the primary school curriculum into just one year and the three-year secondary cycle into 18 months. The programs have been adapted in several states and municipalities, such as Acre, Amazonas, Pernambuco, the state of Rio de Janeiro, and the municipality of Rio de Janeiro. For younger students, the Instituto Ayrton Senna has developed Se Liga to help prevent age-grade distortion by ensuring that children in early grades who have not mastered basic reading skills get extra help. For young children who can read but are at risk of grade failure, the institute developed Acelera Brasil, which delivers two years of content in one year. This program is being used, among other places, in Paraíba, Piauí, Tocantins, and the federal district.

Despite the broad reach of these programs, rigorous evidence of their effectiveness and cost-effectiveness is essentially nonexistent. Anecdotal evidence highlights many success stories but fails to capture high dropout rates in some of the programs as well as (in some cases) high costs. As these initiatives continue to spread, the need for evidence on the effectiveness and cost-effectiveness of different approaches is growing. Rigorous evaluation can help policy makers make smart decisions about how best to improve education results within finite budgets; it enables them to know how much it will cost to achieve certain gains. The highly regarded Poverty Action Lab at the Massachusetts Institute of Technology (MIT) is working to generate this kind of evidence from innovative programs around the world. Figure 22 is an example of this work: comparing the cost of achieving an additional year of schooling via very different types of programs evaluated in places as disparate as Madagascar and Mexico. As we discuss later, Brazil, with more than 5,500 education systems, provides an extraordinary opportunity to learn from a great range of education programs, but such learning is only possible with high-quality impact evaluations that use rigorous methods and common metrics.

Figure 22. Cost-Effectiveness of Alternative Education Programs

(additional years of attendance per $100 spent)

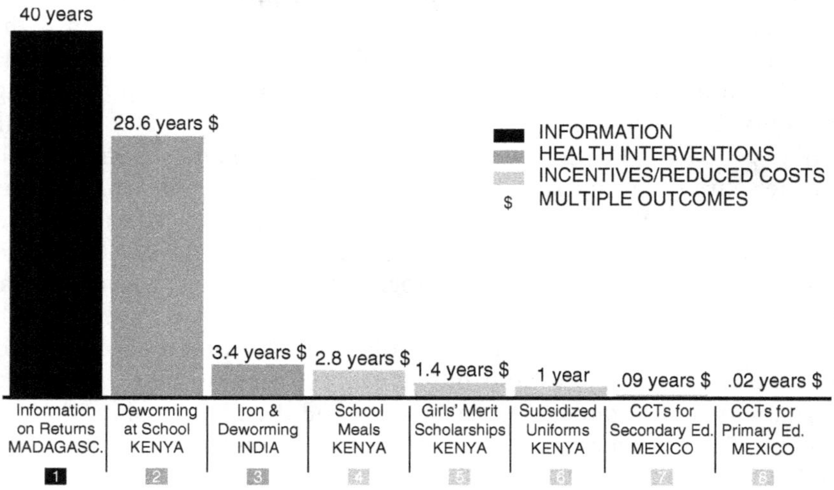

Information on Returns, MADAGASC.	40 years
Deworming at School, KENYA	28.6 years $
Iron & Deworming, INDIA	3.4 years $
School Meals, KENYA	2.8 years $
Girls' Merit Scholarships, KENYA	1.4 years $
Subsidized Uniforms, KENYA	1 year
CCTs for Secondary Ed., MEXICO	.09 years $
CCTs for Primary Ed., MEXICO	.02 years $

Legend:
- INFORMATION
- HEALTH INTERVENTIONS
- INCENTIVES/REDUCED COSTS
- $ MULTIPLE OUTCOMES

Source: www.povertyactionlab.org.

Transforming Spending into Learning

The third critical task of any education system is to transform education financing into results—above all, learning outcomes. We have discussed the major advances in Brazilian education over the past 15 years; now we look at the financing of that progress.

Public Spending on Education As a Share of GDP

Education spending in Brazil was stable in real terms under Cardoso but, after a sharp dip in 2002, has increased rapidly under Lula da Silva (figure 23). Spending per student at all levels of the education system—from crèches to postgraduate universities—is on an upward trajectory in real terms. In 2009, education accounted for 16 percent of consolidated public expenditures in Brazil. In 1995, Brazil's national education spending of 3.7 percent of GDP badly trailed the OECD average of 5.5 percent. But Brazil now spends 5.2 percent of GDP on education, compared with an OECD average of 5.7 percent.

How much spending is enough? Global comparisons provide some perspective. First, while overall education spending for the OECD is estimated at 5.7 percent of GDP, this includes both public and private

Figure 23. Consolidated Education Spending, 2000–2009

(constant 2009 Rs)

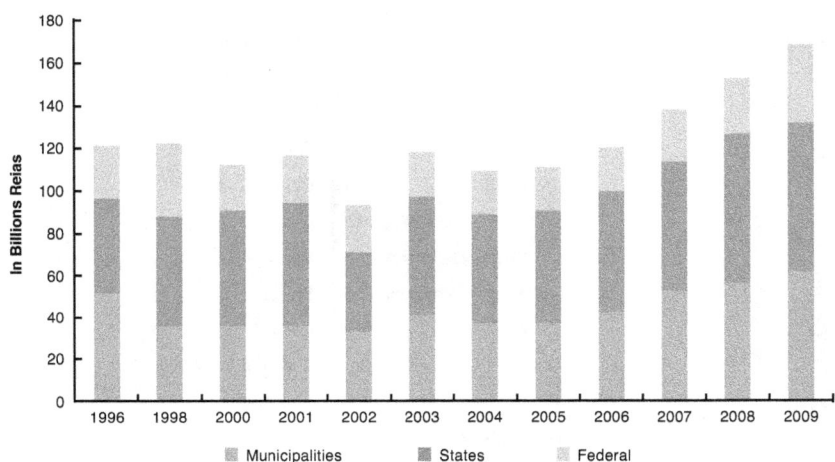

Source: Brazilian National Treasury.

spending. Average public education spending is 4.8 percent of GDP across the OECD. Since data for Brazil do not include private sector expenditure, this is the most direct comparator. Brazil's current level of public spending is above the OECD mean (figure 24). Because the school-aged share of the population is larger in Brazil than in most OECD countries, this is to be expected; however, as figure 24 shows, Brazil also spends a higher share of GDP on public education than Mexico, Chile, India and Indonesia, which have similar demographic profiles.

Second, GDP is growing faster in Brazil than in most OECD countries, so the same national spending share will translate into more resources per student over time. For decades, fast growth enabled Korea to achieve significant improvements in education coverage and quality at a stable share of GDP, and the same phenomenon is occurring in China today.

Finally, and most important, significant variation underlies the OECD averages for both public and total education spending. The key question is how these spending shares correlate with national performance on internationally benchmarked tests such as PISA. Comparative studies have found no clear link. Public education spending in high-performing countries such as Korea, Japan, Australia, the Netherlands, and Canada is below the OECD public sector average, but governments in high-performing Finland and Norway spend more. Some countries that spend well above the average, such as the United States, have seen declining performance on recent rounds of PISA. And some countries that have upped their spending

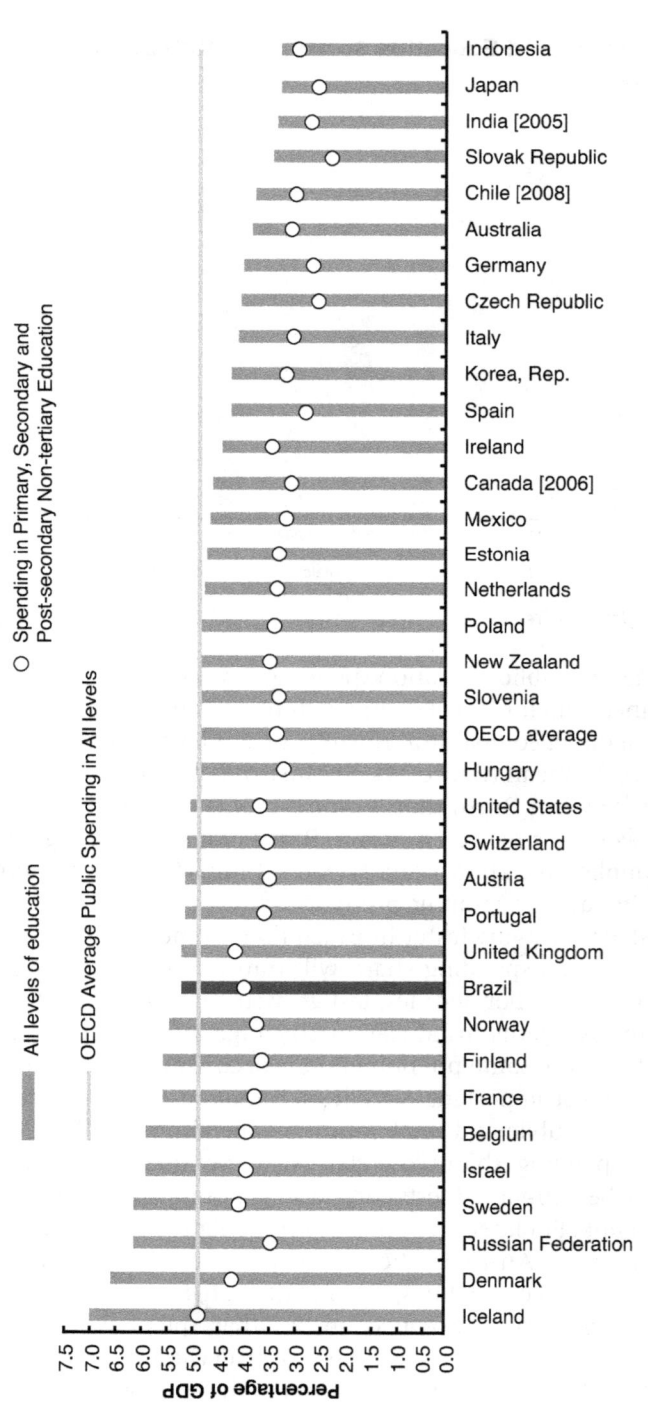

Figure 24. Public Expenditure on Education as a Percentage of GDP in OECD Countries and Brazil, 2007

Source: OECD (2010, table B2.4).

fastest over the past decade (such as the United Kingdom, which increased spending from 4.9 to 5.8 percent of GDP) have not achieved improvements in their globally benchmarked learning results.

Brazil's education ministry and the public-private coalition supporting Educação para Todos (Education for All) have committed to a spending target of 7 percent of GDP by 2015. Union leaders in Brazil call for a national target of 10 percent of GDP. Global comparative data suggest that these levels of investment would be extremely high. The data also suggest that focusing on spending, rather than results, is an uncertain route to progress in education.

The Impending Demographic Dividend

Proposed increases in education spending do not appear to be factoring in the impact Brazil's demographic transition will have on the school-aged population over the next decade. The number of students in primary education tripled between 1950 and 1990, a period of rapid population growth and expanding access to schooling. But since 1990, although coverage has continued to increase, the number of students in primary education has remained approximately 30 million, because the school-aged population has been stabilizing (figure 25).

This will change dramatically after 2012. The 56 percent decline in fertility Brazil has experienced over the past 25 years will begin to produce a radically declining school-age population (Birdsall, Bruns, and Sabot 1996; Wong and de Carvalho 2006). From 2012 through 2025, only the university-aged cohort will remain relatively stable in size; the shrinking number of students at every other level will be felt sharply (table 7). The south and southeast regions will lead in this drop, followed by the

Figure 25. Projected Evolution of Schooling Cohorts, 1990–2025

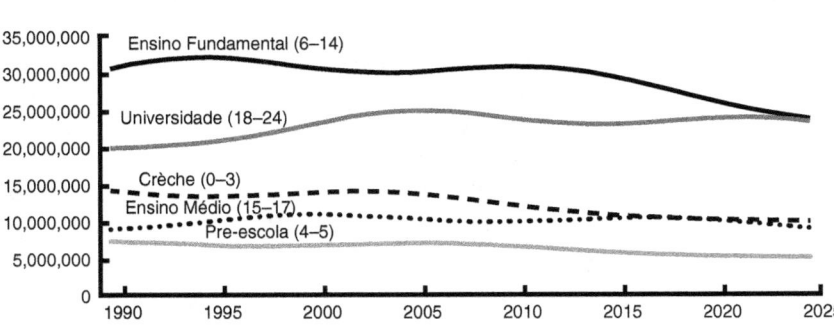

Source: IBGE.

Table 7. Projected Decline in Schooling Cohorts from 2010 to 2025

Level of Schooling	Population Decline (percent)
Crèche	19
Preschool	24
Elementary School	23
High School	10
University	2

Source: Instituto Brasileiro de Geografia e Estatística (IBGE).

center west and, finally, the northeast and north.[11] In primary education, the massive 23 percent drop will mean almost 7 million empty seats in classrooms across Brazil. Were Brazil to follow the Korean example and maintain its current pupil-teacher ratio throughout the transition, the teaching force would decline by more than 200,000 (from 840,000) primary teachers by 2025.

This transition is a dividend for the education system. At similar points in their history, the United States, Japan, Korea, and many European countries used declines in student numbers to shift resources toward quality. In Brazil, some of the resources saved from primary education could support the expansion of crèche care and preschool, which are still far from universal and which research shows are among the best strategies for ensuring that children arrive in primary school ready to learn. It could substantially help finance the expansion of higher quality, full-day schooling at the secondary level. The 7 million empty seats in primary school could also finance investments in quality for the 24 million primary students who will remain.

In sum, population decline and economic growth will generate an automatic increase in spending per student across the Brazilian education system over the next decade without any change in public education spending as a share of GDP. Indeed, without explicit planning for these trends, there is a risk that near-term investments in primary and preschool infrastructure could be wasted. A more promising strategy than targeting increases in education spending as a share of GDP is to focus on the kinds of results other countries have achieved with similar levels of investment. Korea held the share of GDP for education stable during its demographic bonus years from 1970 through 1990, yet registered big improvements in learning.

---

11 Although age-specific population projections by region are not available, the 2000 census suggests this ordering based on the proportions in primary education at that time.

Why Current Spending Isn't Producing Better Results

International comparative data and recent research suggest five areas that are worth examining in pursuit of better results at the current level of education spending:

1. Allocation of spending across education levels
2. Persistent high repetition rates and high costs per graduate
3. Rising teacher costs
4. Little cost-effectiveness research.
5. Corruption and mismanagement of education funds.

Allocation of spending across education levels

This report does not cover tertiary education, and without analyzing the quality or effectiveness of Brazilian tertiary education, it is impossible to evaluate the efficiency of expenditures at that level. But there are obvious anomalies in the allocation of public funds across different levels of education in Brazil compared with other countries. While every OECD country spends more per student on tertiary education than at the primary level—on average, twice as much—the ratio in Brazil is extreme: almost six times as much (figure 26). No other country approaches this figure. The issue is not the share of GDP Brazil devotes to tertiary education; that share (0.75 percent) is well below the OECD average of 1.5 percent of GDP, although for most countries, private spending is a substantial part. The issue is the very small number of students in public higher education relative to spending.

OECD data also indicate, however, that policies have moved in a sound direction since 2000, with a significant increase in the number of public higher education students and a smaller increase in spending, resulting in a 15 percent decline in spending per tertiary student over the decade. Over the same period, spending per primary student rose more than 80 percent. There is little question that government policy is aiming at a better balance, but the staggering disparity in unit costs that remains puts the slow pace of this progress in perspective.

Brazil is also an outlier in its low per student spending at the secondary level. Only a few OECD countries (all from the former eastern bloc) spend less per secondary student than per primary student, but this is the case in Brazil. Unit costs at the pre-primary level are also lower than in primary education, but this pattern is more common.

Secondary education retains the character of an afterthought in Brazil:

Figure 26. Spending per Student at Different Levels Relative to Unit Costs in Primary Education, 2007

Primary education = 100

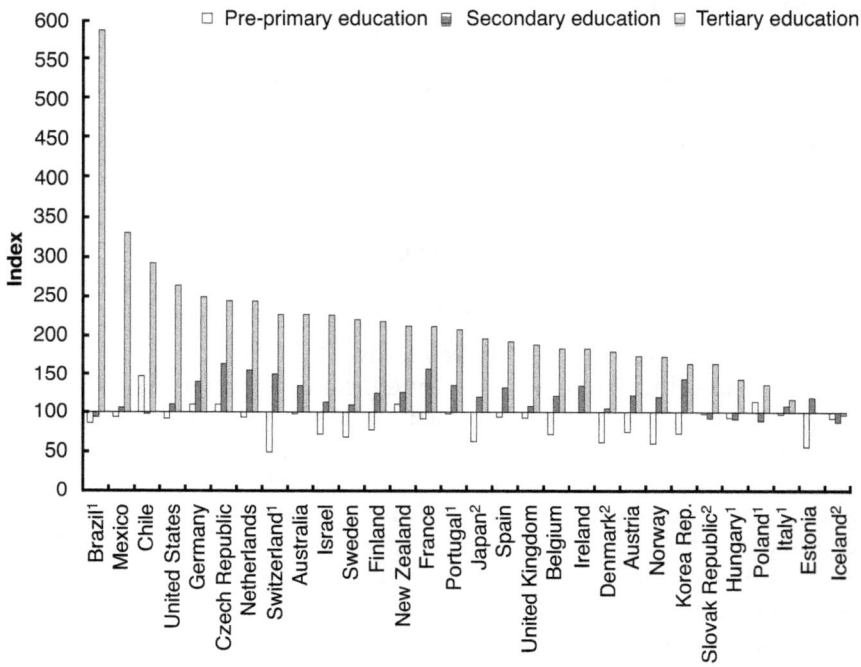

Source: OECD (2010, table B2.4).

Note: Countries are ranked in descending order of expenditure by educational institutions per student in tertiary education relative to primary education. A ratio of 300 for tertiary education means that expenditure by educational institutions per tertiary student is three times the expenditure by educational institutions per primary student. A ratio of 50 for pre-primary education means that expenditure by educational institutions per pre-primary student is half the expenditure by educational institutions per primary student.

1. Public institutions only (except for Italy, in tertiary education).

2. Some levels of education are included with others. For details, see "x" code in table B1.1a,.

night classes in primary buildings, short courses (three to four hours a day), limited availability of laboratories and other facilities. Teachers typically work in several different schools and have little opportunity for joint planning with colleagues, or even for lesson preparation and homework grading. Whether this level of education is preparation for tertiary education or the terminal level of schooling, it should equip students with strong analytical, literacy, and numeracy skills, and the capacity to manage information, solve problems, and continue learning. Most OECD countries are giving this level of education increasing resources and attention; Brazil is lagging in this regard.

Persistent high repetition rates and high costs per graduate

One of the most glaring sources of spending inefficiency in Brazil is the high rate of grade repetition. Many Brazilian students remain in school until age 18—long enough to complete secondary school—but end up having completed only primary education. Brazil has the highest grade repetition rates in the world outside of a very few countries in low-income Africa. International research-based consensus is that repetition is not an efficient educational strategy. Requiring slow learners to repeat grades forces them to spend many hours in school for marginal increases in learning. Although rigorous evaluation evidence is limited, the widely used alternative strategy in other countries is timely remedial intervention during the course of a school year, such as extra tutoring for students who are falling behind. Every school in Singapore has special rooms and a dedicated corps of experienced teachers available to provide one-on-one sessions to students who start to lag until they are back on track. An innovative approach launched by Rio de Janeiro municipality in 2009 is the Reforço Escolar described earlier. All students are tested, and those who are not ready for the next grade receive an intensive two-week learning reinforcement course prior to the start of the next school year.

High repetition is inefficient not only because it wastes students' time and system resources but also because it contributes to higher dropout rates. Approximately 30 percent of Brazilian students drop out before completing primary school, after having stayed in school for 11 years on average—more than enough time to complete the eight-year primary cycle had they not repeated grades. Approximately 25 percent of secondary students drop out before graduating, after having spent four years trying to complete the three-year cycle. Indeed, more than 15 percent of students in Brazil are over 25 years old when they complete secondary school.[12] No other country in the OECD survey has anything close to this extent of age-grade distortion. Brazil's high rates of dropout and repetition contribute to greatly elevated costs per graduate. A conservative estimate

---

12 OECD 2010, table A.2.1, p. 54.

is that the Brazilian education system spends over Rs 11 billion per year (more than 12 percent of total basic education spending) on students who are repeating grades.

Rising teacher costs

In Chapter 3, we consider the central issue of teacher quality. From the standpoint of spending efficiency alone, however, Brazil has pursued several policies over the past decade that have raised teacher costs, with little evidence (either in Brazil or elsewhere) that they contribute to improved results. The first is a policy of lower class size. There has been a consistent decline in the pupil-teacher ratio in both primary and secondary education over the past 15 years. At the primary level, average class size has fallen from 33 in 1999 to 25 in 2008. At the secondary level, it declined from 39 to 30. A decline in the pupil-teacher ratio means an increase in per student costs. Average class size in Brazilian primary education is now close to the OECD average of 22 (figure 27). Efficiency-minded countries such as Korea, Japan, and Chile have resisted this trend; they retain average class sizes of about 30. As the size of the school-aged cohort declines in the coming decade in Brazil, policy makers will have to act to avoid further declines in class size, which increase schooling costs without real promise of better results.

The second policy pursued by Brazil is raising teacher qualifications. The country was an outlier a decade and a half ago, with the very low average schooling level of its teachers, so the increase in teacher salaries and qualifications mandated by the FUNDEF reform was in order. Those policies successfully raised the share of teachers with tertiary degrees from 20 percent in 1996 to 58 percent in 2006 (Menezes-Filho and Pazello 2007). As qualified teachers entered the public sector salary scale at a higher level, the shift in the average level of teachers' academic preparation shifted the wage bill upward.

The issue for education policy makers is the substantial research evidence that teachers' formal academic qualifications have little correlation with their effectiveness in the classroom. When Hanushek, Rivkin, and Kain reviewed 170 estimates of the relationship between teachers' formal education and student performance, 86 percent of the studies showed no significant relationship, and another 5 percent found a negative relationship (Rivkin, Hanushek, O'Brien, and Kain 2005; Hanushek and Kain 2004).

The third policy pursued by Brazil is a secular increase in wages for public sector teachers, on top of the increase induced by higher qualifications. Average teacher salaries have risen steadily compared with salaries for other occupations in the private sector, other occupations in the public sector, and teacher salaries in the private sector (controlling for teacher qualifications

Chapter 2: Brazilian Basic Education: Meeting the Challenge? | 49

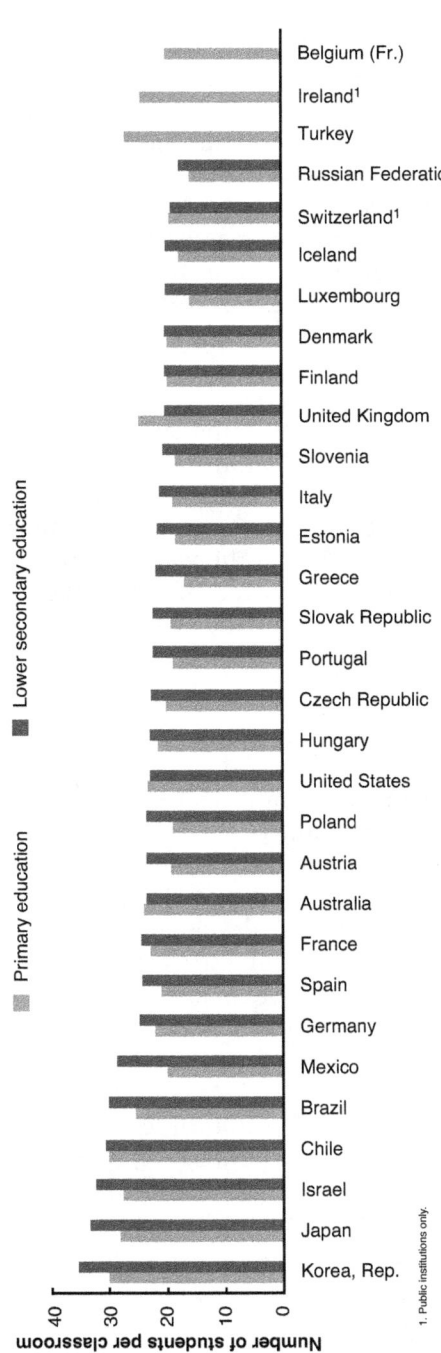

Figure 27. Average Class Size by Level of Education, 2008

Source: OECD (2010, table D2.1). (See annex 3 for notes.)
Note: Countries are ranked in descending order of average class size in lower secondary education.

1. Public institutions only.

and other personal characteristics) (Louzano et al. 2010). Moriconi (2008) found that the 40 percent of teachers who have only a secondary school degree enjoy a substantial wage premium in the labor market, with average pay about 34 percent higher than they could earn in the private sector and 20 percent higher than they could earn as teachers in the private sector. Wages for public sector teachers with a higher education degree still lag those in other sectors, but they also have improved significantly. Whereas in 1995 they were 60 percent below the average wage for a person with tertiary education in other occupations in the private sector, 60 percent below other public sector wages, and 30 percent below the average wage for private sector teachers, the gaps are much smaller today. The essential question, which we address in the next section, is whether the progress made in raising average teacher salaries is enough for a world-class public education system. We note here simply that the significant increase in salaries in real terms has contributed to higher unit costs in education.

All three policies—lowering class size, increasing teacher qualifications, and raising salaries—are among the most common strategies for educational improvement employed around the world. In Brazil, where teacher qualifications and salaries were historically low, these policies were justified. In the next chapter, we explore the question of whether the costs of these policies have been matched by their benefits in education system improvement.

Little cost-effectivness research

Brazil's highly decentralized basic education framework—26 states, a federal district, and more than 5,500 municipal education systems—makes the country a natural laboratory for innovative education policies. Thousands of promising initiatives are launched each year across Brazil. In addition to goverment efforts, a significant number of private foundations are active in program development and providing implementation support to states, the federal district, and municipalities. States and the federal district are beginning to making heavy investments in information technology (e.g., one laptop per teacher, bioscanned fingerprints to digitize attendance) and other large-scale innovations. Most are creatively aimed at Brazil's most serious educational issues, but strikingly few are rigorously evaluated. There is little question that the efficiency of education spending in Brazil could be improved with more cost-effectiveness research, especially if studies were focused on programs of high relevance across different states and results were widely shared.

Corruption and mismanagement of education funds

Research in a number of countries has documented substantial leakage of public funding in the flow from central ministries to front-line service providers, whether schools or hospitals. In one well-documented case, it took concerted government action over eight years to raise the share of education funds reaching schools from 13 percent to 80 percent (Reinikka and Svensson 2005). Public expenditure tracking studies across several developing countries have found that 30 percent or more of centrally allocated education funds fail to reach the schools (Bruns, Filmer, and Patrinos 2011).

No data exist on the extent of education funding leakage in Brazil under the significant number of federal government programs that transfer approximately Rs 5 billion per year in discretionary funding to municipalities, states, the federal district, and even directly to schools for various programmatic objectives. But data do exist on the efficiency of FUNDEF/FUNDEB transfers, which are by far the largest source of education financing.

An explicit goal of the FUNDEF/FUNDEB reform was to rupture past patterns of clientelistic federal funding transfers in education. To do so, FUNDEF instituted a transparent, capitation-based formula for the allocation of education monies across states and municipalities, and established local commissions to monitor how funds were used. FUNDEF's architects sought not only a radical improvement in the equity of education spending in Brazil but also an end to the long-standing culture of public funding exchanged for political support. Evidence reviewed earlier in this report shows that, under FUNDEF/FUNDEB, money has flowed in new directions and education spending has become more equitable.

But many local commissions did not assume the active oversight role federal reformers had envisaged; in May 2003, the federal government launched an unprecedented anticorruption program, introducing random audits of municipalities to track their use of FUNDEF money. Under the program, the Controladoria Geral da União (CGU, Office of the Controller General) uses a public lottery system to generate the names of 60 municipalities each month that are then visited by audit teams for a one-week investigation of their education, health, and infrastructure spending. Researchers Claudio Ferraz and Frederico Finan (2011) exploited this database for an innovative evaluation of the effect of corruption-induced leakage on education outcomes.

The first finding was that funding diversions were widespread. Of the first 790 municipalities audited, the CGU found evidence of corruption in 35 percent, through techniques such as fake receipts, overinvoiced goods and services, and payments made to contractors without service provision. An early CGU report estimated overall funding losses between 13 percent and 55 percent of FUNDEF's total budget (Mendes 2004).

The second finding was that the leakage of FUNDEF resources had direct consequences for the quality of municipal education. Municipalities with detected corruption were much less likely to have adequate school infrastructure or to provide in-service training to teachers. Teachers and directors in these municipalities were more likely to cite a lack of resources as a principal concern. The centerpiece of this research was the first direct evidence that the lower quality of services resulting from corruption had a negative effect on student learning; in municipalities where corruption was uncovered, test scores were on average 0.35 standard deviations lower, and failure and dropout rates were higher. This extent of learning disparity is very large by global standards, where a 0.2 SD difference in outcomes is a large effect.

A large strand of global education research has tried to explain why increases in education spending in many countries have failed to produce better results. Public expenditure tracking studies and the work of Ferraz and Finan in Brazil show the scope for discrepancies between spending allocated to education at the source and funds actually spent on service delivery on the ground. A higher share of GDP allocated to education, in Brazil or elsewhere, will not translate into better learning outcomes unless transparency and management are adequate.

Conclusion

Viewed in a global context, the Brazilian education system of 2011 has already achieved OECD levels of public education spending and is ratcheting up its education results in the area that counts most: student learning. However, several areas of concern should be at the top of the current government's agenda.

First, Brazil is still quite far from the average learning levels, secondary education completion rates, and student flow efficiency of OECD and other middle-income countries. Unless the education system does a better job of preparing a 21st century workforce, Brazil will lose ground in global economic competition to countries with higher skilled populations, such as China. As in every education system, improving teacher quality is the biggest challenge. But Brazil also faces issues in upgrading the infrastructure, instructional hours, curriculum, qualifications framework, and labor market links in secondary education.

Second, while access to education in Brazil has become vastly more equitable over the past 15 years, there is a persistent gap between rich and poor in learning levels and graduation rates. Global research points to early childhood interventions as the most powerful strategy for truly leveling the education playing field. The federal government and municipalities have begun moving on this agenda in a major way in recent years, but coverage rates and quality indicators have a long way to go.

Third, Brazil's highly decentralized basic education system, social interest in education, and new generation of results-oriented politicians are creating a unique public policy landscape. Several states (and the federal district) and municipalities in Brazil are on the cutting edge of global education policy with teacher pay-for-performance reforms (Bruns et al. 2011). Diverse and promising approaches are being developed for early childhood development services, accelerated learning, early grade reading, in-service teacher support, student mentoring, school cohesion in conflict zones, and many other areas. A more active role by the federal government in supporting rigorous evaluation of different approaches and disseminating the evidence could help improve the efficiency of spending across all states, the federal district, and municipalities.

3

Brazilian Basic Education 2011-2021: The Next Agenda

In this chapter, we examine what we see as the four most important challenges for Brazilian education over the next 10 years: (1) raising teacher quality; (2) protecting the early development of the most vulnerable children; (3) building a world-class secondary education system; and (4) maximizing the impact of federal policy on basic education, especially by capitalizing on Brazil's "education action lab."

Building Better Teachers

Teacher quality is the central issue in education policy. While the importance of having a good teacher is intuitively obvious to any parent or student, only over the past decade have researchers begun to quantify how crucially individual teachers affect student learning gains. Over the course of a single school year, students with a poor teacher master 50 percent or less of the curriculum for that grade; students with a good teacher can get an average gain of one year; and students with a great teacher advance 1.5 grade levels or more (Farr 2010; Hanushek and Rivkin 2010). A series of great or bad teachers over several years compounds these effects and can lead to unbridgeable gaps in student learning levels.

The hottest question in education policy and research is how to recruit great teachers and raise the performance of teachers already in service. The key elements sound simple: (1) attract high-caliber people; (2) support continuous improvement in practice; and (3) reward performance. But countries around the world are struggling to put these elements in place. Policy makers in virtually every country confront an empirical reality of teacher recruitment and compensation systems with weak links between salary and performance. The vast majority of education systems are characterized by lifetime job tenure, rigid pay scales, and very flat career progression, with the top teacher salary after 20 years of service usually not even twice that of an entering teacher. These systems create labor environments in which extra effort, innovation, and good results are not rewarded, and there are no penalties for poor performance. The rate of teacher dismissal for poor performance across the OECD is less than 3 percent (Weisberg et al. 2009). We will look at each of these issues in the Brazilian context and review the latest global evidence—some of it from Brazil—on how best to address them.

Recruiting Higher Capacity Teachers

Virtually every school system in the world recruits teachers on the basis of formal educational qualifications and/or certification processes, but research shows that these "observable" factors are not good predictors of teacher effectiveness on the job, measured as the ability to boost student learning (Rivkin et al. 2005). School systems are searching for selection standards that will do a better job of predicting which teachers should be hired and retained. Even in the most sophisticated screening systems, some recruits do not perform as well as expected; there is growing use of induction systems that give newly hired teachers a one- or two-year period of probation, with their classroom performance closely supervised, before making a final hiring commitment. Even longer periods of probation are part of the strategy for raising teacher quality in quickly improving U.S. districts such Boston and Chicago, where teachers are not made permanent until they have been teaching and closely evaluated for three and four years, respectively. Pruning out weaker performers is a significant part of these districts' aggressive efforts to raise the bar for teacher quality. In Brazil, the *residência escolar* being pioneered in the Niteroi municipal system is a move in this direction. Modeled on the years of closely observed practice used for beginning medical doctors, Niteroi's system for a carefully supervised teacher probation period appears promising, although there has been no evaluation of its impact yet.

In general, global research supports the importance of high cognitive skills and content knowledge for effective teaching. Interpersonal skills, character traits such as patience and perseverance, and personal charisma also contribute to the makeup of outstanding teachers. But the *sine qua non* appears to be strong content knowledge. Countries in which new teachers are recruited from the top third of university graduates—such as Korea, Singapore, and Finland—have the best performing education systems.

Who goes into teaching in Brazil? In Brazil, teachers are recruited from the bottom third of students. The country is not alone in this pattern. PISA data from 2006 showed that the average cognitive ability of 15-year-old students who identified themselves as prospective teachers was well below that of prospective engineers in every country except Poland, and below the national average in most countries. (Uruguay was the one exception in Latin America) (see figure 28.) Even though the PISA data show this as a global pattern, its implications are stronger for Brazil, whose overall PISA performance is at the bottom of the skill distribution for its income level.

Brazilian researchers have documented the same pattern: teaching is a low-status profession that does not attract high academic performers. In 2005, only 11 percent of the high school students interested in becoming teachers were among the top quintile of graduating students, while 30 percent were in the bottom quintile. Compared with engineering students, Louzano and colleagues (2010) documented that teacher training students come from significantly poorer and less educated families, and are less likely to attend private high schools.

Figure 28. Comparative PISA Math Performance of Prospective Teachers and Engineers

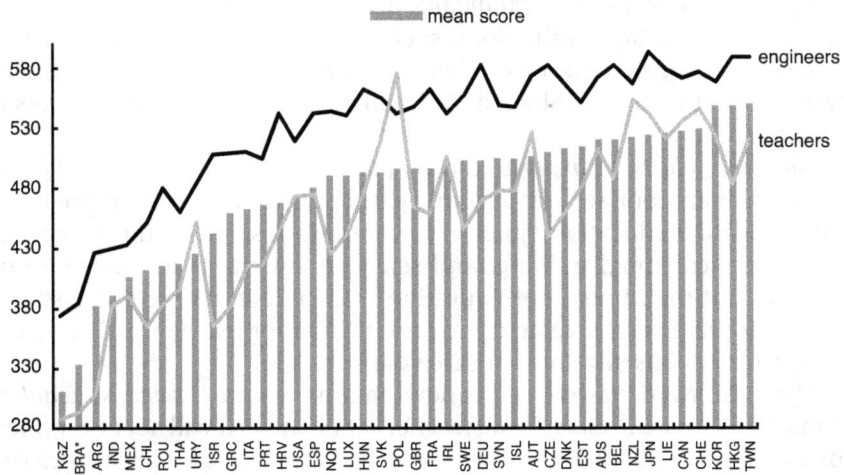

Sources: Brazil results are from PISA (2000); all other countries are from PISA (2006).

It is interesting to observe that the highest performing education systems globally do not always have high teacher wages relative to per capita GDP, but they always have highly selective teacher recruitment processes, in which the number of places in teacher training programs is limited and there is competition for entry. Singapore accepts only 20 of every 100 teacher education applicants. Finland reports nine applicants for each new opening. Selection criteria emphasize academic achievement on university qualifying exams, but candidates are also screened for communication skills and motivation, and observed during practice teaching.

In Brazil, there is no winnowing of teacher candidates at entry to teacher preparation programs. There are many programs, and the number of trainees has continued to grow, although about 70 percent of trainees are people with previous teaching experience who are upgrading their formal credentials. A recent review of a sample of graduates from 532 pedagogia programs found that average institutional quality—measured by student performance on exit exams—was not high. Test scores were highest for teachers with no previous experience who trained in public institutions, but private schools were as effective in training persons with previous teaching experience. The researchers hypothesize that private schools offer a less theoretical curriculum (Louzano et al. 2010).

Teacher selection in Brazil begins after teachers have graduated. The process is highly decentralized; individual states and municipalities set their own criteria and hiring processes. At the state level and in many municipalities, hiring is based on a written examination and a review of formal qualifications, and candidates are ranked. There are typically no interviews or on-task evaluations, such as preparation of a sample lesson plan or teaching a sample class. There may be a probationary employment period, but it is rarely enforced. In smaller municipalities, the process is even less formal.

National policies to improve teacher quality. It would be difficult and probably inappropriate for a country such as Brazil, with more than 5,000 separate education systems, to aspire to a single national teacher preservice screening, training, and selection system as in Singapore or Finland. But the Ministry of Education (MEC) deserves credit for strong actions at the federal level to try to raise the bar for teacher quality across the country. It has developed a threefold strategy.

First, the MEC has created a new national exam *(Exame Nacional de Ingresso na Carreira Docente)* for all teacher candidates. (It will not be required for existing teachers.) The exam covers both content and pedagogy. The national exam is an important step; even though the federal government does not have the authority to revamp the curriculum of university education departments because of institutional autonomy, those departments will be forced to respond to the more stringent requirements of the exam—especially the emphasis on high-level content mastery in math, science, and language, rather than the philosophy- and ideology-dominated curricula currently used in many universities.

The exam seems to be a good compromise between the need for more transparent and comparable information about the skills of teacher candidates across the country and the need for states, the federal district, and municipalities to retain the autonomy to set standards for entering teachers that are appropriate for their particular region or context. The ministry will not mandate any particular score that teacher candidates must attain, and it will not certify candidates on the basis of their exam performance. But similar to the role it has played in providing transparent information about school results through the IDEB, MEC would play an important role in generating a public good (information about teacher competency) that can make state and local decisions more efficient.

Second, to improve preservice training quality, MEC is collaborating with the federal universities to fund 100,000 new teacher positions at top universities across the country; these positions will be for science and math teachers, an urgent priority in Brazil.

Third, MEC is mandating that every state and municipality and the federal district establish a formal teacher recruitment process and a career plan. All recruitment of new teachers must be through an organized and transparent exam (most states already do this, but recruitment in many small municipalities is highly discretionary), and they must establish a clear career path for teachers. Recruitment must be based on subject matter mastery as well as pedagogy and credentials. The career plan must allow the teacher to see the performance requirements for progression as well as for increases in salary.

This effort to establish a higher entry bar for teacher quality is crucially important, and MEC's well-designed policies follow the lead of states such as São Paulo and Minas, which have already put in place rigorous, content-based tests for teacher candidates. In São Paulo, tests of content mastery are also used to regulate the conversion of temporary teachers to permanent contracts.

State-level innovation: São Paulo's Prova de Promoção. With almost 2 million teachers already in service, it would take decades for Brazil to affect the overall quality of instruction solely through higher standards for new entrants. Recognizing this, the state of São Paulo in 2009 adopted an innovative complementary reform—the Teacher Promotion Exam *(Prova de Promoção)*—to create a highly paid career track for top teachers within the current 230,000-person teaching force. Civil service teachers may opt into the new salary scale by passing a difficult test of content mastery. The rewards are high: from an average salary of R 1,830 and top

> **BOX 3**
>
> ## Evaluating the Impact of São Paulo State's Prova de Promoção
>
> São Paulo's innovative effort to upgrade teacher quality by creating a selective, highly remunerated career track is one of a handful of such programs in Latin America and an important potential model for the region, along with Chile's *Asignación Variable por Desempeño Individual* and Peru's *Carrera Publica Magisterial*. The state is collaborating with international researchers to generate evidence on three important policy questions:
> 1. Is there a correlation between teachers' scores on the *Prova de Promoção* and the previous year learning results of their students (i.e., does the evidence support the hypothesis that teachers' knowledge and content mastery is a better predictor of their classroom effectiveness than their years of service or other observable characteristics)?
> 2. How does entry into the new salary progression affect a teacher's subsequent effort and classroom practices?
> 3. Is the existence of the new career path attracting higher caliber applicants into the state school system?
>
> The second and third questions will take more time to evaluate, but to begin examining the first question, researchers mapped the test performance of teachers who took the exam in 2010 with the learning performance of their students at the end of the 2009 school year. São Paulo's excellent administrative data made it possible to link classroom-level student learning results for approximately 3,500 fourth-grade teachers, 6,000 eighth-grade math teachers, and 8,500 eighth-grade Portuguese teachers. In each case, average student performance on the São Paulo standardized test (which aligns with the national standardized assessment) was compared with *Prova de Promoção* scores for the teachers assigned to those classrooms in 2009. The results showed a significant correlation between teachers' level of content mastery and the previous year performance of their students, controlling for teachers' years of experience and level of schooling. This is concrete evidence that two teachers who may look the same on paper, in terms of their teaching experience and academic qualifications, actually perform differently in the classroom. It also provides evidence that teachers whose own mastery of the content is stronger are more effective in helping their students to learn.
>
> A panel of 500 teachers—half of whom barely accessed and half of whom just missed the 20 percent cutoff for entry into the new salary scale in 2010—is being followed for the next two years to analyze how the program affects teachers' satisfaction, expectations, professional development actions, and performance in the classroom. The research proposal includes classroom observations of both groups of teachers.

> **BOX 3** *continued*
>
> One of the most important impacts of the new reform could be its effect on the average caliber of entering teachers. While this can only be analyzed over time, a record number of potential teachers registered for São Paulo's 2010 entrance exam *(concurso)*, mounted after the *Prova de Promoção* was announced: 270,000 candidates for 10,000 openings. Researchers are currently analyzing the median test scores, university preparation, and socioeconomic profiles of the successful candidates and the overall applicant pool in 2010 compared with those of previous years. This may show whether the new career stream, by attracting more qualified candidates into the teaching profession, allows the state to recruit more selectively. The research will also follow both new teachers and new entrants into the Prova de Promoção salary scheme over the next several years to analyze their effectiveness in raising student learning. Although the evidence from OECD countries indicates a correlation between teachers' content mastery and their classroom effectiveness, in terms of producing higher student learning outcomes, there is limited evidence on this from developing countries. The São Paulo study will be an important contribution.

salary of R 3,181 a month in 2010, the highest salary grade under the new structure will pay teachers R 6,270 a month, decompressing the ratio of top-to-bottom teacher salaries from 73 percent to 242 percent. This new top-level salary is the equivalent of four times per capita GDP annually and would place teachers in the top 10 percent of professional salaries nationally. Teachers must earn a high score on the test to qualify for level 1 of the new track (6 or more on a 10-point scale), but the fiscal impact of the reform is also controlled by a tournament rule that a maximum of 44,500 teachers per year (20 percent of the total teaching force) may enter the new career track, in rank order of their performance on the test.

In 2010, more than 96,000 teachers opted to take the test. Of those, 81,000 achieved the threshold score, and 44,589 entered the new system. Teachers must wait three years in any new salary grade before they can compete for the next level, which has a more demanding threshold score. The new policy creates strong incentives for current teachers to continue to acquire content knowledge and for high-capacity individuals to enter teaching. The São Paulo reform not only has clear relevance for other states in Brazil that are grappling with the same issues, it is also one of the best-designed programs of its kind in the world. To help expand the thin global evidence base in this area, the state is participating in a World Bank–supported impact evaluation as part of a cross-country research study of teacher incentive reforms (box 3).

Alternative Certification: Ensina! Brazil is not the only country concerned that its teaching profession has lost prestige and no longer attracts top caliber university graduates. A non-government program called Teach for America arose 20 years ago in the United States to address exactly this issue, and devised an alternative route into the classroom for a new breed of teacher. In response to requests for support from both other OECD and developing countries across all regions, over the past five years an international offshoot under the name Teach For All has begun to spread the "Teach for America" model globally.

The essence of the TFA model is an approach to recruiting, training and mentoring talented young professionals that stands in sharp contrast to traditional teacher recruitment channels. First, Teach For All targets top graduates of top universities – people who typically would not consider teaching as a profession. It appeals to these individuals to make a public service commitment to work for two years as teachers in highly disadvantaged schools. Second, Teach For All follows a distinctive approach to training and mentoring recruits. In contrast to most multi-year, pre-service teacher education programs, Teach For All prepares teachers through a very intensive one month program called the "Summer Institute" and complements this with weekly one-on-one mentoring throughout the two year assignment.

Teach For All's first Latin America offshoot was Enseña Chile, launched in 2008 with its first teacher placements in the 2009 school year. Enseña Peru and Enseña por Argentina followed, with teacher placements in 2010 and 2011, respectively. Colombia and Mexico are currently initiating programs.

In 2010, Ensina! Brasil was established, recruiting a cohort of 32 teachers that began working in 14 of Rio municipality's Escolas do Amanhã in March 2011. The Escolas do Amanhã are located in low income, high conflict areas which are targeted by the Rio Education Secretariat for special support. As in the other Latin America programs, Ensina! attracted a large number of applicants for its initial 32 positions, which enabled the program to be highly selective, focusing on both candidate teachers' cognitive skills as well as their motivation and interpersonal skills. (Table 8).

Unlike most of the other countries, however, Ensina's teachers are not allowed to teach in regular classrooms, because Brazilian policy currently does not allow for alternative models of teacher certification. Ensina's teachers therefore offer reinforcement classes in the afternoon shifts for students falling behind. However, as it is not mandatory for students to attend these classes, the impact of the program is not as substantial as in the other countries, where teachers have a larger number of regular students and spend more time with each class per week. Even so, the initial response to Ensina! from Rio's school directors and students has been highly positive.

Evaluations of the TFA approach in the United States have demonstrated two key results. First, this new breed of teachers can be more effective in raising student learning than traditionally-recruited teachers. In the most rigorous study to date in the U.S., students randomly assigned to TFA teachers improved their math scores compared to students in control classrooms by 0.15 standard deviations (a significant differential) and performed equally well in reading. TFA teachers not only outperformed other novice teachers, but also veteran and certified teachers in the same low-income schools (Decker et al 2004). A 2010 Inter-American Development Bank study followed a less rigorous method but also found positive impacts in both Spanish and math performance of students of Enseña Chile teachers compared to novice teachers in similar schools (Alfonso & Santiago 2010).

A second key result from research to date is that the new breed of teachers differs significantly from traditionally-recruited teachers in their expectations of students. Echoing earlier research results in the United States, the IDB's analysis of Enseña Chile found that while only 30 percent of traditionally recruited teachers were "confident that students with behavioral problems will learn", 49 percent of Enseña teachers believed this. While only 17 percent of regularly-recruited teachers described their classes as well-disciplined (having "few or very few" students that were noisy or distracted), 43 percent of Enseña Chile teachers reported this.

Like the other TFA offshoot programs, Ensina! Brasil is structured as a public-private partnership. All of the program's overhead costs are covered by private philanthropic contributions. Substantial technical support in implementing the model is provided by the international parent NGO, Teach For All, which also raises funding from private philanthropic contributions. The scalability and ultimate impact of the model, however, rests on it being mainstreamed into the regular school system, as in Chile

Table 8. A New Model of Highly Selective Recruitment: Teach For All Programs in Latin America

	Enseña Chile, 2009	Enseña Peru, 2010	Enseña por Argentina, 2011.	Ensina! Brasil, 2011
Completed applications	326	810	398	2,400
Invited to interview	150	256	131	110
Recruited	31	27	14	32
Successfully placed	19	26	13	32

Sources: Inter-American Development Bank (2011) and Ensina! Brasil.

and Argentina. In these countries (and the U.S.), the TFA recruitment and training process is considered a valid alternative certification path and Enseña teachers fill vacancies in regular public schools, drawing a regular salary. Very often, Teach For All teachers have the math and science skills to fill vacancies, particularly at the secondary level, that could not otherwise be filled. At present, Ensina! cannot help meet these needs. Without the ability to supply candidates for vacant positions in regular public schools in Brazil, Ensina's financial viability is unclear.

That is unfortunate, as both the evidence from other countries and the initial experience in Brazil suggest that Ensina's alternative recruitment and supervision model could play an important role in building better teachers in Brazil. First, Ensina! has the potential to help public school systems in many parts of Brazil meet urgent short term needs for higher-skilled math and science teachers. Second, Ensina! represents an innovative approach to teacher recruitment, preparation and mentoring that deserves rigorous impact evaluation. Its "summer institute" may represent a more cost-effective model of teacher preparation than university-based pedagogy programs. Ensina's model of intensive mentoring for new teachers may have a high payoff if extended to regular teachers, as well.

Brazil's public education systems today face huge challenges in raising school quality, above all in disadvantaged communities. In many of these schools, high levels of teacher vacancies have created conditions that justify the label "emergency". It was in response to such conditions that Teach for America, and other alternative teacher certification programs were developed in the US, Chile, Argentina and elsewhere. Allowing states and municipalities to establish reasonable alternative certification standards that broaden the pool of qualified teachers and test out innovative teacher preparation and support programs holds promise for Brazil as well.

Improving Teacher Practice

Whatever the level of teacher quality at entry, education systems all share the challenge of developing the best teachers possible out of the teaching force in place. Part of the issue is motivating teachers to perform, which we discuss in the next section. But many researchers are convinced that, especially in settings where teachers' skill levels are low, even motivated teachers may simply not know how to improve.

The record on in-service professional development leading to measureable improvements in teacher effectiveness is dismal (Borko 2004; Garet et al. 2001; Cohen and Hill 2001). In Brazil, states and municipalities annually outsource a large amount of in-service training to local universities and foundations, and approaches vary widely. We discuss several creative and well-regarded programs in the next section, but none of them have been rigorously evaluated. Many programs are delivered by university education departments that have ideological approaches, including a belief that the low quality of Brazilian education is rooted in the poverty and low development of the students. Reformist secretaries of education have to work hard to counter this culture, using mantras such as "every child can learn" and "if a student isn't learning, it is the fault of the school, not the child."

The highly theoretical in-service training delivered by many Brazilian universities contrasts dramatically with new trends in teacher professional development in OECD countries. There, training is increasingly focused on transmission of concrete, practical strategies and techniques distilled from observing highly effective teachers in action (Farr 2010; Lemov 2010). Inspired by the work of researchers such as Charlotte Danielson (2007), Douglas Lemov, and Teach for America's intensive teacher support program, these in-service programs emphasize several themes: the crucial importance of managing classroom time to maximize instruction, designing lesson plans and pacing activities to keep students engaged, assessing student progress continuously, and targeting help to students who are falling behind.

Leading state and municipal education secretariats in Brazil have begun to adopt this research-based approach to improving school quality. In Minas Gerais, Pernambuco, and Rio de Janeiro municipality, teams of trained observers have used a standardized protocol developed in OECD countries to conduct the first systematic classroom observations in Brazil. They are generating representative classroom-level data on overall system performance and helping to identify highly effective teachers. These observations are proving to be a rich source of information for school-level improvement planning and for the design of concrete, practical teacher development programs.

Some key results of the classroom observations are reported here (tables 9–13). The Brazilian data are highly consistent with OECD experience in one respect: variations in teacher effectiveness from one classroom to the next inside the same school in Brazil are almost as large as the variations seen across schools. Fully 75 percent of the variation in classroom practice observed across a sample of several hundred schools can also be seen within many of those schools. This is a staggering degree of disparity in teacher practice within schools but consistent with what is found in other countries. The implication for policy is clear—and promising. If the "technology" for more effective teaching is already present somewhere in the school, the challenge is to share it more widely, and the costs of doing so are potentially low.

In other respects, however, comparing the Brazilian data with the OECD good practice benchmarks is sobering and provides a window

Table 9. Use of Class Time: Rio de Janeiro, Pernambuco, and Minas Gerais

Use of Instructional Time	Rio de Janeiro Municipal Schools	Pernambuco State Schools	Minas Gerais Pilot Study		OECD Good Practice Benchmarks
			Schools That Improved 2005-2007	Schools That Declined 2005-2007	
Learning activities	62%	61%	66%	63%	85%
Classroom organization	31%	27%	27%	25%	15%
Nonacademic activities	7%	12%	8%	12%	0%
Teacher out of the classroom	3%	8%	3%	6%	0%

Sources: Rio de Janeiro Municipal Secretariat of Education (2010), Pernambuco State Education Secretariat (2009), Minas Gerais State Education Secretariat (2009), and World Bank.

Table 10. Use of Classroom Materials: Rio de Janeiro, Pernambuco, and Minas Gerais

Teaching Materials Used*	Rio de Janeiro Municipal Schools	Pernambuco State Schools	Minas Gerais Pilot Study	
			Schools That Improved 2005-2007	Schools That Declined 2005-2007
No materials	14%	21%	15%	8%
Textbooks	11%	16%	19%	11%
Workbooks and writing books	28%	21%	32%	40%
Blackboard	33%	29%	25%	34%
Learning aids (maps, charts)	9%	7%	7%	1%
ICT (computer, projector, radio)	1%	3%	1%	4%
Cooperative learning activity**	4%	2%	2%	2%

* As a proportion of the total time the teacher was in the classroom engaged in teaching.

**Cooperative learning activities are noted every time a group of students is working jointly on a common task, irrespective of materials being used.

Sources: Rio de Janeiro Municipal Secretariat of Education (2010), Pernambuco State Education Secretariat (2009), Minas Gerais State Education Secretariat (2009), and World Bank.

Table 11. Students Off-Task: Rio de Janeiro, Pernambuco, and Minas Gerais

Activities	Rio de Janeiro Municipal Schools	Pernambuco State Schools	Minas Gerais Pilot Study		OECD Good Practice Benchmarks
			Schools That Improved 2005-2007	Schools That Declined 2005-2007	
Share of time some students are off-task	43%	46%	51%	64%	6% or less
o/w Large group	18%	15%	19%	25%	

Sources: Rio de Janeiro Municipal Secretariat of Education (2010), Pernambuco State Education Secretariat (2009), Minas Gerais State Education Secretariat (2009), and World Bank.

Note: Large group = more than 5 students.

Table 12. Use of Instructional Time in Top versus Bottom Performing Rio de Janeiro Municipal Schools, 2010

Fourth-grade classrooms	Learning Activities	Classroom Management	Non-academic Activities	Teacher Out of the Classroom
All schools in sample	58%	37%	6%	1%
10% of schools with highest IDEB scores	70%	27%	3%	0%
10% of schools with lowest IDEB scores	54%	39%	7%	3%
Difference	0.16	-0.13	-0.03	-0.03
Standard errors	[0,09]*	[0,09]*	[0,02]	[0,01]**
* Denotes significant at the 10 percent level; ** Denotes significant at the 5 percent level.				

Sources: Rio de Janeiro Municipal Secretariat of Education (2010) and World Bank.

Table 13. Student Engagement in Top versus Bottom Performing Rio de Janeiro Municipal Schools, 2010

Fourth-grade classrooms	Percent of total class time some students off-task	
	Large or small group of students off-task	Large group of students off-task
All schools	35%	13%
10% of schools with highest IDEB scores	30%	10%
10% of schools with lowest IDEB scores	50%	28%
Difference	20%	18%
Standard errors	[0.14]*	[0.09]**

Sources: Rio de Janeiro municipal education secretariat and World Bank.

Note: Large group = more than 5 students. * Denotes significant at the 10 percent level. ** Denotes significant at the 5 percent level.

into major issues in Brazilian education. The classroom observations measure four things: (1) how the teacher uses class time, (2) how the teacher uses available materials, (3) what pedagogical practices are used most frequently (e.g., question and answer, lecturing, copying from the blackboard), and (4) student engagement.

Looking at the data from Minas, Pernambuco, and Rio de Janeiro municipality, a few patterns are remarkably consistent:

- *A high share of classroom time is lost.* In the OECD, good practice norms are for teachers to spend at least 85 percent of class time on instruction; no more than 15 percent on classroom administration (taking attendance, collecting homework, cleaning the room, passing out papers); and no time on nonacademic activities (chatting with students, leaving the classroom to get something). In all the Brazilian systems observed to date, time spent on instruction is below 66 percent. Time spent on classroom management (from 25 percent to 31 percent) is much higher than in the OECD, and nonacademic activities absorb 7 percent to 12 percent of the teacher's time. The teacher is outside the classroom from 3 percent to 8 percent of the time—usually either arriving late or leaving early. Since the data collected are representative state-wide, teachers missing from the classroom 8 percent of the time on average means that students in this state lose 16 days of schooling per year from teacher tardiness.

- *Traditional teaching methods predominate.* Books are used less than 20 percent of the time. The blackboard is the principal teaching method used 25 percent to 34 percent of the time. Between 8 percent and 21 percent of the time, no materials are used. Almost no use of information and communication technology (ICT) or cooperative learning activities was observed.

- *Students are not engaged.* Between 43 percent and 64 percent of the time, a small or large group of students (six or more) is visibly off-task (e.g., chatting, texting, sleeping). The OECD benchmark is 6 percent or less.

- *Students learned more when classroom time was used more effectively.* In the top 10 percent of Rio de Janeiro municipality's schools measured on the IDEB, teachers spent 70 percent of classroom time on instruction, compared with 54 percent in the bottom 10 percent of schools. In classrooms in the top schools, teachers did not miss a minute of official class time; in the bottom schools, teachers were absent from the classroom 3 percent of the time.

- *Students learned more when they were engaged.* In Rio de Janeiro municipal schools that scored in the top 10 percent on the IDEB, large groups of students were off-task only 10 percent of the time, compared with 28 percent (more than a quarter of total instructional time) in schools that scored in the bottom 10 percent of the IDEB. Small groups of students off-task were observed in both sets of schools, however.

In each of the school systems observed to date, many classrooms exceeded the OECD good practice benchmarks for time spent on instruction. In some classrooms, students were never off-task. In some classrooms, books, materials, ICT, and cooperative learning activities were used as intensively as in the best schools in Finland, Korea, or Canada. Brazil has many teachers like the "heroes" profiled in annexes 1 and 2. But these teachers and their classrooms are not the norm in Brazil today.

Some teachers resist having their work observed. But dynamic education secretaries such as those in Minas Gerais, Pernambuco, and Rio de Janeiro municipality are moving on many fronts to reform and improve their schools. They believe that reforms can improve student learning only if they create observable improvements in teacher practice in the classroom. Systematic research on classroom dynamics allows the impact of new programs—such as Pernambuco's innovative teacher bonus, Minas's *Alfabetização no Tempo Certo,* Rio de Janeiro municipality's *Educopedia* and *Ginasio Carioca* initiatives—to be measured rigorously over time. It allows education secretaries to identify excellent teachers who can serve as demonstration teachers and in-school mentors. It can provide essential feedback for school-level development plans. Above all, it can support the design of effective teacher development programs by focusing on concrete, high-priority issues and disseminating practical, effective strategies generated from within the system itself.

Motivating Performance

On the other side of the coin, teachers—like any other workers—cannot be expected to develop and apply their skills unless their effort is rewarded. Considerable cross-country evidence shows that teachers respond to various kinds of incentives—not only salaries, pensions, and other pecuniary rewards but nonmonetary incentives as well, such as intrinsic motivation, professional growth, feedback from students, recognition, and prestige (Vegas 2005). In fact, a striking feature of education systems everywhere—in contrast to most other sectors of the economy—is that neither job tenure nor salaries are directly linked to individual results. The wage scale for teachers is typically much more compressed than those in other sectors, and salary increases are almost exclusively determined by seniority and formal credentials, despite global evidence that neither seniority nor credentials are good predictors of teacher effectiveness and that the ability of individual teachers to produce educational results varies widely.

The evidence is less consistent regarding what average salary level is needed to attract high-capacity people into teaching over other professions. The average teacher salary in basic education across the OECD is about 1.2 times GDP per capita. But PISA data show no clear correlation between average salary levels (relative to national per capita GDP) and education system learning performance. Korea and Japan pay above the average, while Finland and Norway pay below. On the other hand, most research literature shows that the widespread pattern of relatively flat salary progression over teachers' careers, plus promotion policies rigidly linked to formal credentials or seniority, combine to create weak incentives for teachers to perform (Ballou and Podgursky 2002; Delannoy and Sedlacek 2001; Odden and Kelley 1997; Umansky 2005).[13]

To address this problem, school systems are increasingly experimenting with "pay for performance" programs that award teachers an annual bonus on the basis of their relative performance. Several U.S. school districts, most notably Washington, DC, are implementing programs of this type (see Box 4). In the developing world, the most ambitious reformer had been Chile, which has both school-based and individual rewards for teachers, based on evaluated performance. Mexico, Peru and India have also introduced various forms of performance-linked pay.[14]

---

13   *OECD's Education at a Glance* (2010) reports that across all OECD countries, average teacher salaries at the top of the scale are only 70 percent higher than starting salaries. Korea is an outlier, with top salaries more than 250 percent higher than starting salaries.
14   See Bruns, Filmer, and Patrinos (2011) for a review of the latest global evidence

> **BOX 4**
>
> ## Holding Teachers Accountable for Performance: Washington D.C.'s IMPACT Program
>
> A radically new approach to evaluating and rewarding teacher performance, called IMPACT, was the signature achievement of the controversial former D.C. Chancellor of Schools, Michelle Rhee. The teachers' union fought its adoption, but the system has survived Rhee's departure and is increasingly viewed as a model by U.S. educators. The Obama administration's $5 billion Race to the Top grant competition made reform of teacher performance evaluation an explicit criterion. At least 20 states, including New York, and thousands of U.S. school districts are beginning to adopt systems that look like IMPACT.
>
> The IMPACT reform had three main goals: i) to bring clear teaching standards to a district that lacked them; ii) to establish a comprehensive annual process for review of teachers' performance, including direct observation of their classroom practice; and iii) to establish outright dismissal as a consequence of ineffective teaching.
>
> The evaluation system leans heavily on student test score gains to judge teachers, such as in math and reading, whose students are tested annually. Ratings for teachers in subjects or grades that are not tested are determined mainly by five classroom observations annually, three by the school principal and two by "master educators," generally recruited from outside Washington. IMPACT costs the city $7 million a year, including pay for 41 master educators, who earn about $90,000 a year and conduct about 170 observations each. The program also asks more of principals. The head of a school with 22 teachers, for example, must conduct 66 observations, about one every three school days.
>
> For classroom observations, nine criteria—"explain content clearly," "maximize instructional time" and "check for student understanding," for example—are used to rate a teacher's lesson as highly effective, effective, minimally effective or ineffective. These five observations combine to form 75 percent of these teachers' overall ratings; the rest is based on student achievement data and the principal's assessment of the teacher's commitment to the school community. Teachers rated highly receive big bonuses. Teachers rated minimally effective have their salaries frozen and are given one more year to improve. Teachers rated ineffective face immediate dismissal. In 2010, 165 Washington teachers were fired. In 2011, a further 200 to 600 of the city's 4,200 educators are expected to be dismissed, the nation's highest rate of dismissal for poor performance.
>
> One of IMPACT's recognized accomplishments has been to align teacher performance with student performance. Indeed, Michelle Rhee's inspiration for the program was the disconnect she observed as Chancellor: "Only 8 percent of D.C.'s 8th graders were on grade level in

> BOX 4 *continued*
>
> math, and only 12 percent in reading—yet the vast majority of teachers were 'exceeding expectations' on their end-of-year performance reviews." Now that the program is in its second year of implementation, it still has critics, but many teachers report the feedback received from master educators and school directors has improved their practice. Jason Kamras, the architect of the system under Chancellor Rhee, said "it's too early to answer" another early criticism—that IMPACT makes it easier for teachers in well-off neighborhoods to do well. But Washington's compensation system offers bigger bonuses ($25,000 versus $12,500) and salary enhancements in high-poverty schools.

But Brazil is currently one of the world's most important venues for pay for performance reforms in education, for several reasons. First, at least fifteen state and municipal systems have launched bonus programs, and several are already in the second or third year of implementation. Second, although the programs share common objectives and are all linked to IDEB performance measures, they have different design features (e.g., average bonus size, how the targets are set) that affect the strength of the incentive. Third, and most important, because of the unique opportunity to generate global knowledge from the ongoing Brazilian experience, several leading states are collaborating with international researchers to study these design differences in a systematic way. The impact evaluations under way in Pernambuco, São Paulo, Minas Gerais and Rio de Janeiro municipality constitute the deepest and most extensive comparative research program on this topic in the world at present.

While all four programs award annual bonuses to teachers and all other school personnel on the basis of the school's performance against annual targets, the rules for setting the targets are most conducive to rigorous evaluation in Pernambuco and in Rio de Janeiro municipality.[15] With slight variations across the cases related to the possible evaluation methods, researchers are analyzing how the introduction of bonus pay affects (1) school outcomes (student learning and progression rates as

---

regarding teacher incentives.
15 In Minas Gerais, school targets are set through negotiations between regional administrators and individual schools. In São Paulo, the bonus is structured as a continuous function of a school's achievement of its targets; for example, if a school achieves 10 percent of its target, personnel receive 10 percent of their monthly wage as a bonus. In Pernambuco, the rules for setting the targets are based on the quartile of the performance distribution into which each school falls. This has created discontinuities in the targets that permit rigorous evaluation of their effects; for example, two schools will have more or less ambitious targets depending on where they fall in the cutoffs.

measured by IDEB); (2) teacher effort, attitudes, and teamwork/social capital within the school; (3) possible adverse behaviors (cheating, teaching to the test, diversion of school time from nontested to tested subjects and grades); (4) schools' strategies for improvement; and (5) parents' ability to hold school directors accountable for results (in Pernambuco, school directors are elected by the community). Of the four cases, the evaluation in Pernambuco is the most advanced, so we share here the initial results from that case.

Pernambuco's teacher bonus program. In 2009, Pernambuco launched a highly innovative pay for performance system that rewards school personnel for achieving their annual school improvement targets. All schools that achieve at least 50 percent of their targets receive a proportional bonus, up to a cap of 100 percent; for example, if they achieve 60 percent of their targets, each member of the school staff (teaching and nonteaching) receives 60 percent of the average bonus (prorated for his or her salary level) in additional pay. Since the state budgets one month's education payroll for the program annually, the average bonus will exceed one month's salary if less than 100 percent of schools achieve it. In the first year of the program, 52 percent of schools achieved their targets, and the awards averaged 1.8 months of salary. In the second year, 79 percent of schools received the bonus, and the average award was 1.4 months of salary. This is a large incentive compared with other programs internationally. Pernambuco's rule that schools achieving less than 50 percent of their targets receive nothing is also a strong incentive. In São Paulo, by comparison, every school receives some bonus.

The strength of the incentives in the Pernambuco design make it an important case to analyze. The research is ongoing, so results reported here are preliminary, but the following are key findings thus far (Ferraz and Bruns forthcoming):

- *Acceptance of the bonus program was relatively high.* Sixty-four percent of school directors surveyed in the first year of the program believed the policy was appropriate, and 66 percent reported that the bonus program was having a positive impact on their school—whether or not they actually received the bonus.

- *Schools with more ambitious targets achieved more progress.* In almost every performance category (4th, 8th, or 11th grade; math or Portuguese), schools that fell on the "higher target" side of the performance cutoffs made larger test score gains than comparison schools just below the cutoffs. The differential learning gains were sharpest for schools just above the 25th percentile of performance. For the eighth grade in 2008, for example, schools on the higher target side of the cutoff improved their average test scores in Portuguese by 31 percent of a standard deviation more than schools just below the cutoff (with less ambitious targets). In math, the performance differential was 15 percent of a standard deviation. At the second cutoff (just above and just below the 50th percentile in the performance distribution), improvements were also higher for the schools with more ambitious targets but were of a smaller magnitude. For the other tested grades (4th and 11th), impacts were in similar ranges but varied across subjects and, in a few cases, by cutoff point. Overall, the evidence was consistent: at least over the very short term, higher targets in the presence of an attractive incentive in Pernambuco resulted in higher learning results by schools.

- *Learning levels across the state improved significantly.* Pernambuco state schools as a whole registered significant average learning improvements, especially in Portuguese. Average Portuguese scores in 8th and 11th grade increased from 2008 to 2009 by 44 percent and 57 percent of one standard deviation (SD), respectively. Math scores in 8th and 11th grade rose by 27 percent and 31 percent of one SD. These learning gains are very large compared with observed results from other teacher incentive programs. However, since this was a universally applied program in the state, these are raw gains, not gains relative to a comparison group. Difference-in-differences analysis will be needed to bound the gains. Pernambuco ranked quite low in national IDEB rankings in the previous year (2007), so some of these gains likely reflect a natural tendency of unusually low or high scores to revert to the mean.

- *Schools that just missed receiving the bonus for 2008 appear to have improved more than schools that barely achieved the bonus for 2008.* A key research question is whether schools that received the bonus in 2008 would be more motivated in 2009 or would exert less effort and coast. To examine this, the performance of schools that fell just short of 50 percent of their 2008 targets (and did not receive the bonus) was compared with the performance of schools that achieved just over 50 percent of their targets and did get the bonus. Controlling for 2008 test results and other characteristics, schools that barely missed the bonus in 2008 improved more than schools that barely achieved the bonus in 2008. It appears that just missing the bonus had a positive effect on schools' motivation and performance, at least in the first round.

- *Schools whose teachers spent more time on instruction were much more likely to achieve the bonus.* Classroom observations carried out in November 2009, just before the end-of-year student achievement exams, showed significant disparities in how efficiently teachers used classroom time for instruction (table 14). These differences—and differences in the share of

Table 14. Classroom Dynamics in 220 Pernambuco Schools, November 2009

Teachers' Use of Instructional Time	OECD Good Practice Benchmarks	Overall Sample	Earned Bonus for 2009	Did Not Earn Bonus for 2009	Difference, Bonus and Non-bonus Recipient Schools
Learning activities	85%	61%	62%	53%	0.09 [0.04]**
Classroom management	15%	28%	27%	30%	-0.03 [0.03]
Teacher off-task	0%	12%	10%	17%	-0.07 [0.02]***
Teacher out of classroom	0%	8%	8%	12%	-0.04 [0.02]***

Sources: Bruns, Cruz, and Amorim (forthcoming).

Note: Standard errors in brackets: * significant at 10 percent level; ** significant at 5 percent level; *** significant at 1 percent level.

time teachers were off-task or absent from the classroom—were highly correlated with a school's likelihood of achieving that year's bonus (paid in 2010 on the basis of year-end performance in 2009).

A joint team of Pernambuco and international researchers is currently exploring the in-school factors that may explain consistent success, as well as how the targets and bonus payments interact to induce school improvement. Periodic observation of more than 1,800 classrooms in 300 schools is shedding new light on why some schools perform better than others and how incentives affect school actors. In theory, if a pay incentive causes an improvement in student learning, it should operate through changes in teacher behavior that are induced by the incentive, such as increased or more effective teaching effort. It will be interesting to see how these patterns evolve over time after schools become more familiar with the program and react to the information of either achieving or not achieving the bonus during 2010.

The evaluation of Pernambuco's pay for performance program is expected to continue for several more years, permitting much deeper analysis of how annual targets and past rewards affect schools' improvement strategies, teacher behaviors, and overall system progress. The results of the evaluation will be directly comparable to results for the bonus program adopted in 2010 in the municipality of Rio de Janeiro, which also sets targets for improvements in IDEB outcomes as the basis for the bonus and also has established performance targets around several different thresholds. The Rio program design is additionally interesting because it embodies strong sanctions against teacher absence: only employees with five or fewer absences for the school year (whether excused or unexcused) can receive the bonus. In 2010, 290 of Rio de Janeiro's 1,044 municipal schools qualified for the bonus on the basis of their 2009 IDEB improvements, but more than a fourth of these schools' 11,000 employees did not meet the bar for individual attendance. Rio de Janeiro municipality's program is currently the strongest effort to attack endemic absenteeism in Brazilian schools. It will be important to measure how the bonus program's incentives affect absence rates over time.

As in Pernambuco, a large sample of Rio de Janeiro municipal schools is being followed in a panel study that includes systematic classroom observation using standardized protocols. Although the evaluations of the Minas Gerais and São Paulo bonus programs cannot exploit the same research methods, similar data are being collected and will enrich the comparative analysis. A set of dynamic education secretariats in Brazil, pursuing innovative policies and willing to subject them to research scrutiny, are currently pushing the frontier of global knowledge on pay for performance in education.

Strengthening Early Childhood Education

Children with identical cognitive performance at age three can develop large advantages or delays in development, depending on the wealth and educational level of their families. These disparities in the cognitive potential and skills of children from advantaged and disadvantaged backgrounds become more acute over time, as demonstrated by cognitive development measured by a vocabulary test in Ecuador (see figure 29).

Early childhood development (ECD) programs have powerful potential to compensate for inequalities in income and social background. Evidence from the United States suggests that high-quality ECD programs have significant effects on cognitive ability, earnings, and social behaviors. Across several programs, the educational impacts are clear and consistent. Grade retention is reduced between 13 percent and 47 percent, the likelihood of secondary school dropout is reduced between 24 percent and 32 percent, and some programs show increased college participation. Beyond education to the life outcomes that matter most, a variety of programs have demonstrated important long-term social impacts—significantly reducing involvement in crime, adolescent pregnancy, and drug problems, and significantly augmenting earning potential (Barnett and Belfield 2006).

Figure 29. Cognitive Development of Children Aged 36-72 Months in Ecuador

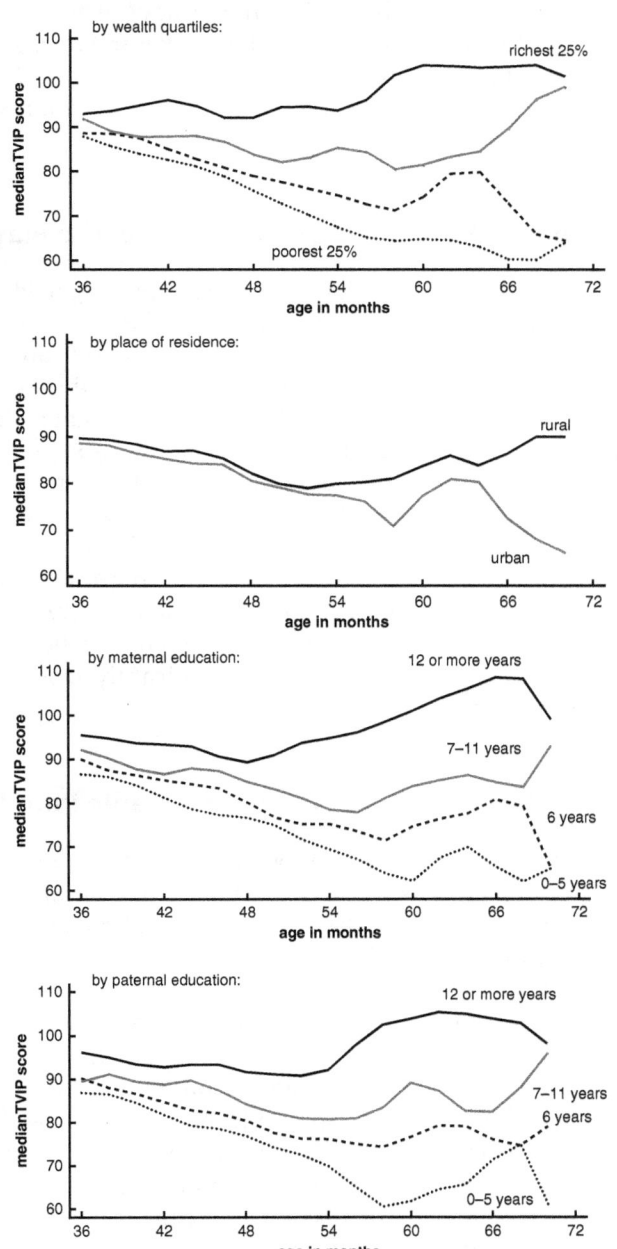

Source: Paxson & Schady (2007).

The returns from these early intervention programs tend to dramatically overshadow returns from programs for older children, suggesting that expanding investment in early childhood education is wise. Evidence on the subsequent schooling progress of children exposed to early education suggests that the impacts are complementary, making later education investments even more effective. Early childhood education strengthens the quality of the entire system.

Improvements in Access and Quality to Level the Playing Field

Whether early childhood education can level the playing field depends on the access disadvantaged children have and whether ECE has differential impacts for them. Because many studies have focused on the poorest children, there is limited evidence regarding the relative impact across income groups. However, two studies in the United States demonstrate larger cognitive effects for disadvantaged children, and some evidence from international studies (Ecuador, Mauritius, Vietnam) suggests the same (Nores and Barnett 2010). Further, because disadvantaged children are particularly at risk for adverse social outcomes (e.g., involvement in crime and adolescent pregnancy), impacts in these areas may be significantly higher for them (Barnett and Belfield 2006). However, simulations suggest that only large improvements in both access and quality for the most disadvantaged can significantly close the gaps in school readiness (Magnuson and Waldfogel 2005).

High-Quality Programs That Reach Vulnerable Populations

Not all early childhood education programs are equal, and the clearest evidence of positive impacts comes from programs that are high quality and well targeted. For example, the Perry Preschool Program in the United States included (for three- and four-year-old children), a daily 2.5-hour program as well as weekly home visits by teachers. The program had a clear, active learning curriculum in which children planned, carried out, and reflected on their activities (Heckman et al. 2010). The Abecedarian program, also in the United States, offered full-day child care (up to 10 hours daily) for children from three months of age until school entry, also with a clear learning curriculum (i.e., not merely child care) (Barnett and Masse 2007). Both programs targeted highly vulnerable children, and both showed significant developmental benefits for children who participated.

Larger scale programs have shown mixed results. The expansion of public day care provision for children from infancy to four years old in Quebec, Canada, demonstrated small adverse effects on children's social behavior and health (Baker et al. 2008). In Denmark, universal provision of public preschool for three-year-olds had no clear impact on their cognitive or behavioral development (Gupta and Simondsen 2010). In Argentina, a large expansion of public preschool (ages three through five) had positive effects on both test scores and behavior (Berlinski et al. 2009). From this array of evidence, what stands out is that while universal programs may have mixed impacts, programs focused on the most vulnerable children can have unambiguously positive impacts.

Various studies in Brazil have examined the impact of early childhood education, but in most of these studies, it is difficult to completely separate the effect of program participation from other differences. One World Bank study examined outcomes for Brazilian adults who attended preschool between 1937 and 1976 and found positive impacts on total educational attainment and grade progression (World Bank 2001). A more recent study that examined students in one municipality in São Paulo state on the Provinha Brasil in 2008 found that students who had attended preschool or crèche had 6 percent higher literacy scores (De Felicio, Menezes, and Zoghbi 2009).

Improvements in Access

In recent years, Brazil has made great strides in expanding access to early childhood education (ECE), both at the preschool level (ages four through six) and at the crèche level (infancy through three years old) (table 15). Furthermore, ECE has been institutionalized through the 1988 constitution that recognizes it as the right of every child, the 1996 formalizing of responsibility for ECE under the Ministry of Education, and the 2009 constitutional amendment making schooling obligatory from age four (with a gradual implementation through 2016).

While these improvements in policy and expansions in coverage are positive moves, the children who need these programs the most are

Table 15. Improvements in Access to Early Childhood Education in Brazil, 1996-2009

	Enrollment (percent of relevant age group)	
	1996	2009
Crèche	8%	18%
Preschool	49%	81%

Source: Evans & Kosec (2011).

still the least likely to benefit from them. Preschool participation for the poorest quintile of the population lags behind that of the richest quintile by almost 20 percent (75 percent for the poor, 94 percent for the rich), and crèche participation for the poorest is barely one third of that for the richest (12 percent for the poor, 35 percent for the rich).

These wealth distinctions largely overlap with the urban-rural gap, which is even more striking. In 2009, less than 9 percent of rural children were enrolled in crèches, while over 20 percent of urban children were enrolled. Examined together, poverty and living in a rural area each reduce a child's chances of participating in early childhood education (Evans and Kosek 2011).

Access for the Poorest

Providing access to ECE for the very poorest children, especially in rural areas, means supporting creative solutions to the challenge of large distances and sparse population. Providing centers and transport for the youngest children in rural areas may be neither effective nor viable from a budget perspective.

Two states have embraced home-based models as the most viable ways to provide effective services in a rural setting. Both models support early childhood development, although one is housed in the education secretariat while the other is housed in the health secretariat. The example in education is Acre's *Asinhas da Florestania* program. Because four- and five-year-olds cannot be expected to travel many miles through the forest to a school, the state has developed a program to fill the gap as participating municipalities develop their own capacity. The program uses a strategy of home-based visits to support children's social, psychomotor, and cognitive development. Education agents trained by the state secretariat of education, usually high school graduates from the same municipality as the children, visit the homes of the children in rural areas twice a week. The agents usually select one house in the community and gather all the children in the neighborhood. While activities are targeted toward children of preschool age, younger siblings are also invited to participate.

Financing is shared by the state and the municipalities: the state education secretariat provides training, teaching materials, and technical support, and the municipalities pay for their agents and supervisors. The communities are very isolated and very small; they have, on average, five families and five to seven children. The program, launched in 2009, currently serves about 2,100 children.

The example in health is Rio Grande do Sul's *Primeira Infância Melhor* program, which was inspired by Cuba's *Educa a Tu Hijo* program. The program focuses on children from infancy to six years old in areas with high social vulnerability and a lack of early child care and education facilities. For children from birth through 2 years 11 months, the program adopts an individual approach. Children and caregivers are visited for an hour each week by a home visitor, who explains the stimulation activity, helps the caregiver carry out the activity, discusses the child's development as observed in the activity, and answers questions. Families receive materials to help them continue the activities during the week. For children age three to six years, the children and their caregivers meet in a public space (such as a town hall, playground, or a spacious room in someone's home) once a week and carry out a similar agenda as in the home visits (Schneider and Ramires 2007). The program, launched in 2003, currently reaches more than 88,000 children.

States and municipalities can partner to invest in creative programs for children in difficult-to-reach areas. Also, the Ministry of Education can encourage states and municipalities to explore alternatives to center-based care in settings where constructing dedicated centers may not make fiscal or developmental sense, taking advantage of homes and existing structures to offer stimulation for vulnerable children.

Improvements in Quality

Simply providing a place for children to receive care does not automatically result in cognitive development. The quality of the care is paramount, and this is the likely cause of mixed results in many large-scale early childhood development interventions. As Brazil expands access to help the poorest receive cognitive and social stimulation, it must ensure that quality improves. A recent study in six state capitals around Brazil (Belém, Campo Grande, Florianópolis, Fortaleza, Rio de Janeiro, and Teresinha) examined the quality of pre-primary institutions in 18 to 30 institutions per state, using adaptations of two internationally established instruments, the Infant/Toddler Environment Rating Scale-Revised (ITERS-R) for crèches and the Early Childhood Environment Rating Scale-Revised (ECERS-R) for preschool. These instruments measure quality across a broad range of characteristics, including personal care, activities, interaction, space and equipment, program structure, the teaching of speech and comprehension, and faculty and parent involvement (Campos et al. 2010).

Overall, 50 percent of crèches surveyed were judged to be inadequate and only 1 percent were rated good (figure 30). At the preschool level, quality was slightly better: only 30 percent were rated inadequate and 4 percent were rated good. While the Brazilian adaptation involved a shift in scale, making comparisons imperfect, a recent study in 692

Figure 30. Distribution of Crèches and Preschools in Brazil by Quality

(percentage of facilities surveyed)

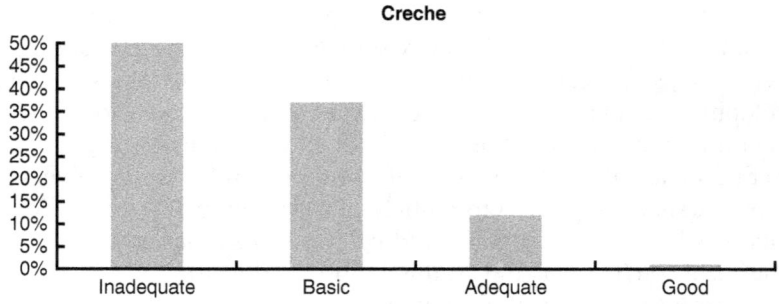

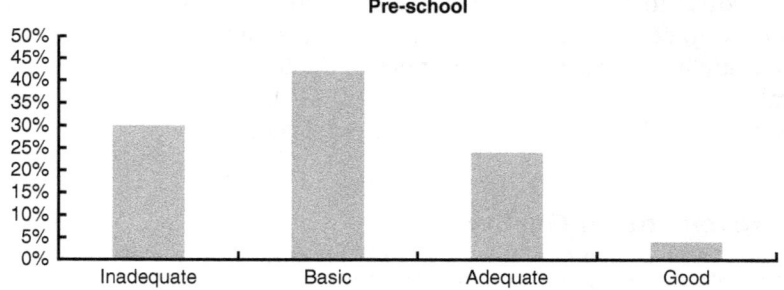

Source: Campos et al. (2010).

American preschools placed the average American preschool squarely in the adequate range (LoCasale and others, 2007). A study of preschools in Germany and Portugal using a comparable instrument also found the average preschool to be of adequate quality (Tietze and others, 1998). What is clear is that Brazilian preschools are significantly lower in quality than their OECD counterparts, and a Brazilian crèche is even more likely to be inadequate.

These ratings point to important areas for improvement. At both levels of education, the weakest areas were activities for the children (e.g., blocks for play, music and movement activities, activities that demonstrate nature and science principles) and program structure. Interactions between staff and children rated relatively highly. In other words, staff want to work with the children but lack the skills and structure to effectively stimulate their cognitive and social development.

Evidence from Rio de Janeiro shows significant disparities in quality across crèches, as well as an overall need for improvement. Using a measure similar to that described on previous page, the bottom 20 percent of crèches in Rio de Janeiro had a level of quality roughly half that of the top 20 percent, and the high-quality centers cost 79 percent more to run per child than the low-quality centers (Barros et al. 2010).

Three key areas determine the quality of ECE programs: curriculum, training and supervision, and ongoing monitoring and evaluation. In each of these areas, the Ministry of Education can play a role in providing guidelines, materials, and oversight. However, core responsibilities rest with the municipalities that implement programs.

- *Curriculum*

In the examples of high-return ECE programs, such as Perry Preschool and the Abecedarian program, a high-quality curriculum guided the activities of caregivers and children. A randomized trial comparing three curricular models for three- and four-year-olds demonstrated far better long-term outcomes with a curriculum in which children initiated activities and teachers responded or teachers and children planned activities together compared with a more scripted curriculum (Schweinhart and Weikart 1998). Many municipalities in Brazil lack any curriculum for early childhood education, and almost all lack a curriculum for crèche care. A crèche-level curriculum should be different from that for preschool, not seeking to transform crèches into small schools but rather providing caregivers with clear instruction on how to initiate activities that will stimulate their children's social and cognitive development. The Basic Education Secretariat in the Ministry of Education offers numerous publications to guide crèches, including a three-volume curricular reference guide published in 1998, and in 2009 the National Education Council published a set of guiding directives for ECE curricula. A natural extension of those references would be a practical guide to daily stimulation activities that municipalities could adapt to their needs.

- *Training and supervision*

The overwhelming body of evidence suggests that high levels of general education are not the key requisites for an effective early childhood educator (Early et al 2007). Rather, it is the belief that each child can grow and succeed, and the ability to focus on a child's needs and facilitate child-centered activities, that make a person an effective caregiver or ECE teacher. Evidence from the United States shows that creative play facilitated by teachers and positive social interaction with teachers can enhance cognitive performance in early childhood education. These principles should be included in preservice and in-service training for early child care-givers.

Evidence from Bermuda suggests that staff with specific training in early childhood education have more positive social interactions with these children (Arnett 1989; Howes and Smith 1995). A review of training systems for ECE workers in three countries revealed that all of them require significant proportions of the staff to have specialized training (see table 16). Brazil's Ministry of Education can encourage municipalities to employ higher proportions of caregivers with specific training in early childhood education and to supplement Proinfantil, the federal program which provides specialized distance training to teachers in crèches and preschools.

Table 16. Early Childhood Education Training in Denmark, France, and Sweden, 2000

Country	Proportion of Caregivers Trained in ECE	Length of ECE Training
Denmark	Two-thirds	3.5 years
France	Age birth to 2 years: at least half	1 year
	Age 3-6: almost all	5 years
Sweden	Preschool teachers: 60%	3 years
	Childcare assistants: 35%	3 years

Source: Moss (2000).

Supervision is essential to enable teachers to successfully apply these principles; it should include regular in-class observation by experts coupled with real-time feedback. More and more education secretariats are adopting direct, systematic classroom observation to monitor and improve primary education; the same systems (using different instruments) are needed in early childhood education. The Ministry of Education could support municipalities in adapting and implementing ECE observation instruments such as the Early Childhood Classroom Observation Measure (which focuses on teacher practices) and the Early Childhood Environment Rating Scale (which focuses on classroom environment and activities).

- *Monitoring and evaluation systems*

No system is perfect. The best programs regularly evaluate what is working and what is not, and update accordingly. In these programs, evaluation is not merely a tool to confirm foregone conclusions but rather an instrument for continual reshaping. An excellent example is the municipality of Rio de Janeiro. In November 2009, in the face of massive demand and a limited supply of crèche care, the education secretariat introduced a new program, *Primeira Infância Completa*, which offered Saturday child care and parenting classes to households on the waiting list for full time weekday crèche care. Despite an initially positive reception, interest in the program waned, as many parents decided that the effort to bring their children to the crèches and participate in the parenting classes was not worth the one weekend day of care provided. In response to real-time monitoring of the response, the education secretariat decided to close down the program and develop an alternative program that provided parenting classes for the most vulnerable households, those benefitting from Bolsa Família, with a small stipend attached. Such willingness to rethink programs that are not effective and experiment with new programs is essential for long-term success.

The municipality of Rio de Janeiro also has put systems in place for rigorous evaluation of programs. In another response to the massive excess demand, the municipality implemented a lottery to give all children the possibility of receiving crèche care, although a higher share of overall spaces are were allotted to the most vulnerable children. The lottery, implemented to fairly distribute limited crèche vacancies, also enabled the direct comparison of children participating in crèches with those on the waiting list. An ongoing impact evaluation of both children exposed to Rio crèche care and those on the waiting list will be the first rigorous evaluation of the impact of crèche care in Brazil, and one of the first in all of Latin America. In 2010, the municipality replaced the lottery system with a means-tested system to take advantage of the targeting data employed in its social assistance program Cartão Carioca.

Schooling a 21st Century Workforce: Raising Quality in Secondary Education

No segment of the Brazilian education system crystallizes the quality gap between Brazil and the OECD countries as clearly as secondary school. Despite high initial enrollments, barely 60 percent of Brazilian youth complete secondary school, compared with 80 percent in OECD countries. In the United States, the 12 percent of high schools that have dropout rates over 40 percent have been dubbed "dropout factories". Using this benchmark, 40 percent of state secondary schools in Brazil qualify as "dropout factories"; in five states, over 50 percent demonstrate this abysmal level of performance (annex table 6.16). Perhaps even more extraordinary is the high share of Brazilian students who do not drop out but spend years pursuing graduation, despite recurrent repetition and the high opportunity costs of remaining in secondary school into adulthood. An estimated 44 percent of Brazilian secondary school students are at least two years overage for their grade, and 15 percent of secondary graduates are over age 25—seven years behind the official graduation age (OECD 2010). Nothing like these patterns is observed in OECD countries or in other LAC and middle-income countries.

Visit a Brazilian secondary school, and in many cases you are entering a school at night (table 17). Korean and Finnish students have a long school day beginning at 7:00 a.m., in buildings replete with labs, laptops, libraries, and performing arts facilities. A Brazilian secondary school may run from 6:00 to 10:00 p.m. in a primary school building, with desks too small for teenaged bodies. Support facilities are rudimentary at best, walls are covered with graffiti, and the halls are unevenly lighted. Teachers, hurrying from their day jobs, may arrive late, and like many of their students may be exhausted.

Table 17. Share of Secondary Enrollment at Night in State Schools and IDEB Ranking, 2009

State	Night Enrollment	IDEB Ranking
Over 50 percent		
Piauí	57%	2.7
Amazonas	51%	3.2
Pernambuco	51%	3.0
Maranhão	51%	3.0
Sergipe	51%	2.9
Below 35 percent		
Rio Grande do Sul	34%	3.6
Rondônia	34%	3.7
Espírito Santo	30%	3.4
Acre	24%	3.5
Roraima	21%	3.5
Distrito Federal	17%	3.2
Brazil	**42%**	**3.4**

Source: INEP (2009).

Note: The National Institute for Education Studies and Research (INEP) defines "night classes" as those starting at 5:00 p.m. or later. All data are for students in state systems.

In the past, Brazil's secondary education system consisted of high-quality university preparatory gymnasiums for the elite and an "S" system of vocationally oriented schooling for the lower-middle classes: SENAI (National Service for Industrial Apprenticeship), SENAC (National Service for Commercial Apprenticeship), and SENAR (National Service for Agricultural Apprenticeship) (Schwartzman 2010). Over the past 20 years, Brazil's massive expansion of coverage has created a new and badly resourced "third leg" of the system: low quality public secondary schools. State secretaries of education across Brazil are working hard to raise quality, but achieving world-class education at the secondary level in Brazil will be a challenge for the next decade. Major infrastructure investments are needed to support a longer school day and eliminate evening instruction. The curriculum, which Schwartzman says is "overloaded with a large number of mandatory courses (including sociology and philosophy in addition to mathematics, physics, chemistry, biology, Portuguese, English, and Spanish, among others)," is impossible to cover effectively in the limited instructional time (Schwartzman 2010, p. 9). Delivering the advanced math and science instruction that OECD countries are emphasizing is complicated in Brazil by a severe shortage of qualified teachers in these areas—virtually every state system currently relies on underqualified temporary teachers to fill the vacancies. And the low content mastery that characterizes Brazilian teachers in general creates acute constraints on academic quality at the secondary level.

Despite the challenges, innovative reforms and good practice approaches are spreading. Some states have achieved large reductions in the share of students in night classes over the past five years. For Brazil as a whole, the share of secondary students enrolled at night fell from 49 percent to 42 percent between 2005 and 2009, but in Tocantins it shrank from 61 percent to 36 percent, and the state's IDEB ranking rose from 2.9 to 3.3 (see table 10). Starting from a much more favorable position, the federal district also achieved a large reduction—from 32 percent to 17 percent—and a subsequent increase in its IDEB ranking. Paraíba, Minas Gerais and Mato Grosso also made substantial progress. Paraná, which scored highest in the country on the 2009 IDEB for secondary education, has developed an impressive program called *Escola Pública Integrada* (EPI, Integrated Public School). Launched in 2003, EPI provides full-day education as well as a broad curriculum, including sports, arts, and culture.

Table 17 does not show a perfect correlation between states' secondary school IDEB performance and either the current level of night enrollment or trends over the past five years, probably because day shifts do not always mean longer hours of instruction. Few secretaries of education believe they can achieve world-class secondary schools without full-day instruction. A comparison with the highly regarded federal technical schools and private secondary schools drives this home (table 18). Although the selectivity of both the federal technical schools and private secondary schools clearly plays a role in their superior learning results, it is no coincidence that these schools also function with longer hours of instruction and almost exclusively by day.

Table 18. Distribution of Secondary Enrollments by Type of School and Shift, and PISA Math Scores, 2009

	Morning	Afternoon	Night	PISA Math Scores
School system				
State	42%	16%	42%	372
Federal	78%	20%	2%	521
Private	88%	8%	4%	486
Brazil	**48%**	**15%**	**37%**	**386**

Sources: INEP Censo Escolar (2009); PISA database (2009).
Note: Morning shift classes start between 6:00 and 11:00 a.m. Afternoon shifts start at noon and end at 5:00 p.m. Night shifts start at 5:00 p.m. or later.

Over the next decade, Brazil's demographic transition will put wind in the sails of a move to full-day secondary schooling. The number of secondary students currently attending night school (3.2 million) is substantially smaller than the projected 7 million student decline in the primary school population before 2020. This will generate major opportunities to reconfigure primary school infrastructure to create full-day secondary schools. Progress in reducing repetition and age-grade distortion could also have a huge impact. Brazil already has a gross enrollment ratio in secondary education of over 100 percent, which means it has enough school places for the entire official secondary age group, even though less than 75 percent of children attend secondary school and less than 60 percent complete it. The difference is that enrollments are swollen with repeaters. As states' strategies for reducing age-grade distortion and improving overall quality begin to make headway, the infrastructure challenges at the secondary level will ease.

But large investments in the quality of school infrastructure will be required. The typical Brazilian secondary school is vastly underresourced against any global comparator. The federal government is investing significantly to expand its network of technical schools. States are developing creative strategies to partner with private corporations to create demonstration schools (discussed below). But only 182 of Brazil's 22,666 secondary schools are federal technical schools, and full-day schools at the state level accommodate only about 10 percent of total secondary students.

A number of states are working on comprehensive strategies. Some, such as Minas Gerais, are developing new approaches to a key issue for secondary education: the balance between academic and vocational content. Although none of the experiences we describe below have been rigorously evaluated, they represent promising directions. They can be loosely grouped as follows:

- Systemwide strategies for improving secondary education

- Demonstration schools

- New models of technical/vocational education.

Systemwide Improvement Strategies

São Paulo. The state of São Paulo offers a good example of a comprehensive approach pursued with sustained political commitment. The state, which has seen its IDEB at the secondary level increase from 3.3 to 3.6 since 2005, has registered even stronger results at the primary level, which should translate into further secondary education improvement in the coming years. The core of the strategy is systematic attention to fundamentals.

First, the state's major reform of the curriculum in 2007 set clear learning standards for each grade and subject at the primary as well as secondary level and launched the development of high-quality learning materials for students and teachers. This has been the anchor for other reforms. It is impossible to have instructional quality without clarity about what is important to teach. International curriculum specialists who have reviewed the state's *Ler e Escrever* and *São Paulo Faz Escola* materials rate them highly.

Second, in the mid-1990s São Paulo was the first state to address the problem of high repetition and age-grade distortion through accelerated learning programs. Although repetition rates have declined (in part through teacher development courses focused on refuting the belief that excellent teaching means high rates of student failure), the state continues to offer well-designed, targeted programs aimed at students who have fallen behind.

Third, for over a decade, the state has emphasized the construction of full-day secondary schools and has reduced the share of secondary students in night schools from close to 70 percent in 1995 to 44 percent in

2009. Although there is still a long way to go, the current administration has transformed an additional 500 schools into full-day schools.

Fourth, from 2008 through 2010, innovative reforms discussed earlier (pay for performance and tests of teacher content mastery) have created incentives for school improvement and a higher threshold for teacher quality across the system.

Fifth, in 2010, the state launched a partnership with three state universities to develop a wholly new approach to in-service training for secondary school teachers, called REDEFOR (São Paulo State Teacher Training Network). The new training is aligned with the curriculum and focused on effective teaching practices, including efficient use of instructional time and full use of learning materials. The one-year course—delivered through the state's 91 distance learning sites to 30,000 teachers a year—represents a new model of in-service training that merits careful evaluation. By specifying the training design and establishing a consortium of university providers, the state has assumed much greater direct control of the training content and quality than has been the norm in Brazil.

A final innovation also serves as a cautionary tale of the difficulty of sustaining education reforms. An innovative language voucher program launched in 2010 permitted São Paulo state secondary students to take one year of intensive English, Spanish, or French instruction at any certified language academy they chose. The innovative program capitalized on the abundance of language institutes, such as Berlitz, that have long catered to private demand. Students could take courses on their own schedules, and the quality of the instruction was considered superior to that available in the state schools themselves. However, the program was not popular with the teachers' union, which viewed it as a threat to its own stock of foreign language teachers. After a change of political leadership in 2011, the program was cancelled.

Ceará. Ceará has also implemented a number of strategies to improve secondary school quality. First, although most schools are still on double shifts, the state has established 59 full-day schools since 2008, with 52 more planned. These schools operate from 7:30 a.m. to 5:00 p.m. and offer both strong academic and technical/vocational course options. Through a joint program with local industry, graduates can take advantage of six-month internships at a state-subsidized wage. After the internship, a graduate may opt to stay in the workforce or move on to higher education. The Ceará schools are a good example of what is considered best practice in the OECD: ensuring that students at all points in their education are qualified to move back and forth from the labor force to the formal schooling system. A major issue with vocationally oriented schooling in many parts of the world has been the low academic content, which left students unprepared for further formal education.

Second, the state education secretariat created a program, a program called Learning First, designed to reduce repetition and dropout rates in the first year of secondary school. The program is based on a set of learning resources to strengthen students' basic math, reading comprehension, and problem-solving skills. It used Ministry of Education support to create teachers' guides and student workbooks for several disciplines and distribute them to all high schools in Ceará.

Third, the state implemented a campaign to upgrade secondary school infrastructure. The highest priority has been ensuring that all secondary schools have science laboratories and sports facilities.

Fourth, the state has improved the skills of high school teachers, particularly in grade nine. Recognizing that part of the reason for high ninth grade repetition rates was teachers' concern that students lacked the appropriate skills, the secretary of education began working with the teachers to convince them that providing struggling students with focused support would be more effective than failing them. To make this strategy viable, the secretariat developed a special training program to help ninth-grade teachers in all disciplines work in a coordinated way on strengthening students' reading comprehension and vocabulary development. The secretariat moved teacher training funding to the school level so teaching teams could set their own priorities and work on them together.

Finally, the state has been more aggressive than most in using IDEB to monitor school performance and holding principals accountable when performance is poor. For its lowest-performing secondary schools, Ceará has hired new principals and given them a portfolio of data on the schools' past performance. Each school has had to prepare an improvement plan and submit it to the secretary for approval. Implementation of the plan is monitored by superintendents on a bimonthly basis. To further stimulate improved performance, the secretariat has created incentives for the 150 best-performing schools to partner with the lowest performing schools. The high performers receive additional funds to support their own school's development plan, but in order to receive the last 33 percent of their funding they must work with a low-performing school to help it improve as well. This innovative "twinning" support complements the other resources the state is channeling to underperforming schools, such as additional training, technical assistance, and instructional materials.

Minas Gerais. The state of Minas Gerais is a further example of efforts on many different fronts to improve the quality of secondary education. One of these—strengthening technical and vocational training—is discussed in a later section. The state has long been the leader in Brazil in school-based management: school directors are elected by the community; schools have control of their own budgets; and school-level planning is a well-developed function. Minas Gerais has complemented autonomy at the school level with an exceptionally effective central administration. The state's central and regional offices provide oversight and support, including curriculum standards, learning materials, teacher training, and, since 2007, a teacher bonus program.

A particularly interesting example of the state secretariat's innovative management is the ninth-grade assessment program, Programa de Avaliação do Aprendizagem Escolar (PAAE) developed in 2008. The PAAE is an ingenious online item bank of test questions developed by teachers and vetted by state secretariat test experts, covering all areas of the ninth-grade curriculum: arts, biology, physics, geography, history, foreign languages, Portuguese, math, and chemistry. The questions are ranked by level of difficulty; the item bank currently includes more than 25,000 questions, including 9,462 easy ones, 11,042 average ones, and 4,129 difficult ones. By logging into the system, a teacher can generate a two-hour test that measures students' mastery of the curriculum for that area. Online feedback from teachers and students who have used the test is highly positive regarding its usefulness and the quality of the test items.

The PAAE is designed to provide confidential, real-time feedback to individual classroom teachers regarding the learning levels of their students at the beginning and end of the school year. The teacher is also expected to take the test. Since it is applied in individual classrooms for individual subjects, the PAAE results represent the true value-added learning gains each teacher produces—they measure exactly what a teacher and his or her students know about the subject at the beginning of the school year and what they know at the end.

Demonstration Schools

A common approach to school system improvement is the establishment of a small number of exceptionally well-resourced schools as "islands of excellence": such schools can test innovations and demonstrate to the rest of the system that high-quality education is achievable. The federal government's highly regarded network of technical schools can be considered an example of this approach.

Pernambuco's escolas de referência. In 2007, Pernambuco partnered with a group of companies committed to improving education to convert 10 existing secondary schools into a new model of full-day schools with high-quality instruction. By 2010, the program had expanded to 60 full-day and 100 half-day secondary schools; by 2011, it reached 174 schools in total. Phillips, Odebrecht, ABN Amro/Real Bank, and Hidreletric Company of São Francisco created the Instituto de Co-responsabilidade pela Educação

(ICE, Institute for Co-responsibility for Education) in Pernambuco. Under the new management model, the state government is responsible for staff salaries, school feeding, books, and uniforms, and the ICE finances infrastructure investments and scholarships for low-income students, and works with school administrators on results-based management. School staff and students are constantly monitored and evaluated during the school year. Teachers receive special support from master teachers for planning lessons and developing instructional materials. A formal state/institute co-management model is used to run the program. Although the program as a whole has not been evaluated, the 2009 IDEB performance of the 51 *escolas de referência* in the SAEB sample for Pernambuco was 4.9, well above the state's average of 3.0. However, the crucial question for Pernambuco—and other states embracing this approach—is how the islands of excellence will translate into systemwide improvement.

Jovem de Futuro

Another promising approach is being supported by the Instituto Unibanco. Jovem de Futuro (Youth of the Future) is a creative program to improve the quality of public secondary schools by promoting school autonomy and results-based management. Participating schools receive technical and financial support to design and implement their own school improvement strategy. Each school receives a grant of Rs 100 per student per year in incremental financing (roughly 10 percent of annual costs per student) to support the plan, as long as it aims at achieving a 40 percent reduction in student dropout and improvements in average math and Portuguese scores (on the SAEB standardized tests). Schools have autonomy to choose from a broad menu of interventions in constructing their plans, ranging from incentives for teachers, to new computers, building upgrades, learning materials, extracurricular cultural activities, or reinforcement classes. The program has been piloted in four states (Rio Grande do Sul, Minas Gerais, Rio de Janeiro and São Paulo) in a total of 86 schools, reaching 69,000 students.

In impressive contrast to many other initiatives in Brazil, Jovem de Futuro has been subjected to a rigorous impact evaluation. In the two first states to adopt the approach—Rio Grande do Sul and Minas Gerais—low-performing secondary schools meeting the eligibility criteria were randomly assigned into the program or into a comparison group. A 2011 evaluation of program impact after three years of implementation showed highly encouraging results. While all of the basic characteristics of the treatment and control schools at the beginning of the pilot were virtually identical, by year three the Jovem de Futuro schools had achieved the target reductions in dropout rates as well as a striking improvement in math and Portuguese performance. As the lead researcher, Ricardo

Paes de Barros, has noted, perhaps the most encouraging aspect of the program is that it has demonstrated improvements in school outcomes in very different state contexts and in the absence of system-wide reforms. In other words, Jovem de Futuro has achieved a proof of concept: there is substantial space for better education outcomes within current political and administrative constraints, simply by infusing schools with a marginal increase in discretionary resources and the autonomy to determine how to use these.

Technical and Vocational Education

One of the biggest challenges in every country is ensuring a smooth transition to work for secondary education graduates who do not go on to higher education. Public-private partnerships can be enormously helpful in orienting the vocational content of the curriculum toward skills that are in demand and supporting results-driven school management, as in Pernambuco.

In Rio de Janeiro state, the Pão de Açúcar Group has helped the state develop a full-time technical education nucleus leading to certification in the food industry for 600 students. Núcleo Avançado em Tecnologia de Alimentos (NATA, Center for Advanced Food Technology) provides full-day education that will include a regular curriculum of secondary education and technical classes.

In Minas Gerais, the Programa do Ensino Profissionalizante (PEP, State Vocational Education Program), an innovative voucher program, is the largest scale and perhaps most promising approach to date. In 2007, in an effort to diversify and expand the technical and vocational training options for youth and young adults, the state launched the secondary-level voucher. Under the program, the state pays the tuition for students to attend any state-accredited training program, whether offered by a private school, municipal school, or industry- based center. The courses are typically 14–24 months long and often organized in partnership with employers, which helps guarantee the relevance of the skills being taught. Many of these partners also commit to hire the graduates over the next five years. A good example is the new training center in Sete Lagoas that specializes in metal mechanics and electronics.

In its first two years, the PEP stimulated the development of new courses in 350 of the state's 853 municipalities and increased the number of accredited training institutions from 72 to 296. By 2009, 25,000 students were taking PEP courses. Establishing quality standards for technical and vocational training programs can be a challenge, given the diversity of providers and training content, but it is essential for success in equipping students with skills that are truly marketable. The Minas Gerais state education secretariat has established a serious accreditation process: of 174 institutions reviewed in 2009, 32 were not approved. If quality is maintained, the program should be cost-effective, as it has induced existing private schools and training centers to expand their enrollments, which makes better use of existing capacity rather than duplicating such capacity in the public sector. In 2010, 158,000 students applied for the 28,000 places available in PEP courses. Schools have an incentive to help students stay in school and succeed academically: the education secretariat transfers voucher payments to the institutions every two months on the basis of an audited report of the number of students and their attendance.

As the first students graduate, their transition to the labor market will be the most important indicator of the success of the PEP approach. So far, the high demand from students, the rapid supply response from the private sector in generating new training places, and the diversity of vocational and training courses generated in the space of two years are impressive. The record of state-run technical and vocational training in Brazil and many other countries is poor; courses are often relatively expensive (because they recreate industrial equipment in a school setting) yet of low quality (because both equipment and faculty quickly grow out of touch with the labor market). Minas Gerais appears to have found a creative and pragmatic way to avoid these problems by combining the relative strengths of the public sector (accreditation, quality assurance, and funding equalization) and the private sector (labor market relevance and flexibility).

Maximizing Federal Impact and Capitalizing on Brazil's Education Action Lab

The "managed revolution" of Brazilian education began when the Cardoso government assumed critical normative functions that had previously gone unfilled: equalizing funding across regions, states and municipalities; measuring the learning of all children on a common yardstick; and protecting the educational opportunity of students from poor families (Souza 2005). With those reforms, the first comprehensive legal framework for basic education (the Lei de Diretrizes e Bases in 1996), and the first national curriculum guidelines, the Ministry of Education got the core elements of a national education policy profoundly right.

Over the past 15 years, this framework has been maintained and expanded, perhaps most impressively in the strengthening of INEP into the LAC region's most effective system for assessing student learning and monitoring education results. Other examples of the strong normative role developed by the federal government over the past two administrations are standards for teachers; high-quality federally supported teacher training programs; a mandate that meritocratic recruitment processes be used in every school system; and the new federal proposal for a standardized teacher entrance exam that could be of great benefit to smaller states and municipalities. The ministry has expanded its core support roles in textbook screening and production, and the funding of high-quality federal technical schools. Finally, the ministry has consistently supported educational innovation: the FUNDESCOLA program to encourage school-level development planning, the *Escola Ativa* to transmit an effective model of multigrade teaching, and the more recent PAR program to strengthen municipal school systems. Brazil's consistent improvement in student learning is in large measure the result of progressive, effective federal policies over a sustained period.

In this context, it is not easy to identify federal policies that could substantially speed Brazil's progress toward world-class basic education. The analysis in this report suggests four key areas.

Stay the Course on Current Federal Policy

Close reading of the data suggests that the pace of educational progress slowed somewhat after the government transition in 2003, which might be expected. However, as discussed throughout this report, under the second Lula da Silva term, the most critical lines of federal education policy were strengthened and extended in important ways. The result has been the impressive improvements in educational outcomes—IDEB and PISA—chronicled in this report. President Rousseff inherited an institutional framework for sustained progress in basic education that has been built up over 15 years. An encouraging signal of continuity is that Lula's education minister has remained in the Rousseff administration.

Focus on Spending Efficiency

The broad-based national commitment to improve education supported by the *Todos Pela Educação* movement and the growing number of private industry groups investing in demonstration schools and other initiatives are positive developments. But the emphasis in public education debates on increased spending is not. Brazilian public spending on education is already relatively high, and the impending large decline in the size of the school-aged population is an opportunity to speed the pace of quality improvement at current spending levels.

Higher spending is not negative per se; the problem is that higher spending in the absence of careful management can worsen the risks of leakage and corruption. Recent cases of overinvoiced and fraudulent education contracts in Amapá and Tocantins echo the earlier comptroller general (CGU) audit report that estimated that 13 percent to 55 percent of FUNDEB funds failed to reach the classroom because of corruption. Clearly, there is room to derive better results from current education spending through strategies to reduce corruption. Expanded random audit programs at the federal level and communicating transparent information about funding entitlements to parents at the school level are two of the best strategies. The impact of corruption on the education system is known; research by Ferraz and Finan (2011) cited earlier in this report found evidence of significantly lower test scores and higher repetition rates in randomly audited municipalities with detected cases of corruption. The mechanisms were clear: fewer resources for teacher salaries, training, infrastructure improvements and computer labs actually arrived at schools, because funding was creamed off at the top. There is little reason to think that higher budgetary allocations—which can have the effect of relaxing funding pressures and lowering vigilance—would redress this type of leakage rather than exacerbate it.

Poor management of education resources—or irregularities in the use of funds without malfeasance—is another issue that cannot be solved by spending more. CGU auditors documented municipalities using FUNDEF and FUNDEB funds mandated for teacher salaries to pay other municipal workers, as well as countless failures to follow competitive bid rules. While not contributing to private gain, these practices also divert resources from education and lower the efficiency of education spending. On the other hand, states, the federal district, and municipalities report instances of poorly managed federal programs, such as two-year delays in the delivery of textbooks, even longer waits for infrastructure programs, and botched implementation of the 2009 secondary school exit exam.

If the current administration makes improving the impact of existing spending a priority, the case for subsequent budget increases, should they be necessary, will stand on far firmer ground.

Create Incentives for Statewide Improvement

Brazil has a long tradition of direct funding relationships between the federal government and municipal authorities that have historically helped cement political alliances. In education, however, there is little evidence that direct support from the Ministry of Education to municipal education secretariats is an efficient strategy for systemwide improvement.

This is not to say that testing new education initiatives on a pilot scale in selected municipalities cannot be useful. The federal government's FUNDESCOLA program to encourage more autonomous schools was launched in 1999 in a pilot set of municipalities that provided an efficient platform for testing the concept in different regional contexts in a manageable number of schools.

But it is striking how many federal education programs focus on direct relationships with municipal education systems rather than the obvious alternative: empowering states to be responsible for statewide educational improvement. The most recent example is the federal PAR program, launched in 2009, which offers direct technical assistance to the 200 worst performing municipal school systems. The objective is laudable: to support low-performing municipal education secretariats as they develop comprehensive improvement programs. However, the modality is questionable: dispatching trained technical teams from Brasilia to distant, sometimes tiny (20 or fewer schools) municipal education systems.

The evidence suggests that the most efficient strategy for improving overall results is closer integration of state and municipal school systems. Many state secretaries observe that "our students come from municipal pre-primary and primary [grades one through four] schools; either we help improve those schools, or we spend time and resources remediating education deficits when their students come into our schools."

Many of the states making the greatest progress in improving education results are those that work most closely with their municipal school systems. While most states are moving in this direction, Minas Gerais and Ceará stand out. Minas Gerais has long made its PROEB (fourth and eighth grade of ensino fundamental and third year of secondary education) and PROALFA (third-grade reading) student assessments available to all municipalities, and the participation is virtually universal. The state's high-quality teacher training programs are also always offered to municipal teachers, and the majority of teachers attend. The state provides municipal schools with the same textbooks and learning materials it uses in its own schools. Above all, the strong program to strengthen early grade literacy teaching *(Alfabetização no Tempo Certo)* has been implemented statewide, in a coordinated effort with municipal school systems. On the 2009 Prova Brasil, the state had the highest fourth- and eighth-grade Portuguese scores in the country.

Ceará also recognized that the problems of low learning levels and high grade repetition start in preschool and the early grades of primary school. Almost a decade ago, the state established an innovative matching fund for the construction of early childhood centers, which are a municipal responsibility. For every center built by a municipality, the state funded an additional center; for the poorest municipalities, the matching ratio was even more generous. The state also worked with municipalities in a coordinated effort to strengthen early-grade literacy teaching, convincing 100 percent of municipalities to sign on to its program. Like the Minas Gerais program, Ceará's program provides training for teachers, along with a revamped curriculum, reading materials, lesson plans, and regular student progress assessments to ensure more effective reading instruction in the first two grades. The state contracted an external testing agency to create an annual reading exam that is given to every second grader in the state, starting with a benchmark assessment in 2007. It has also trained all state and municipal first grade teachers in how to conduct periodic formative assessments of children's reading progress, aligned with the goals of the grade two assessments.

Ceará's statewide strategies for improving educational outcomes have extended to other grades and subjects; they include collaboration on multigrade teaching, support for school development planning, meritocratic processes for selection of school principals, and incentives for teachers. In every case, the state's philosophy is to offer support that municipalities can choose to accept or not. High take-up rates indicate that many small municipal education systems lack the technical capacity to launch programs with the quality and coverage of those the state can mount. The rise in Ceará's fourth grade IDEB results from 3.2 in 2005 to 4.4 in 2009 shows that both systems gain from integrated state-municipal improvement efforts.

Most other states are also moving in these directions, but the Ministry of Education could substantially speed this progress by developing explicit federal-level incentives for statewide improvement strategies. An interesting example is the new U.S. government program Race to the Top (RTT). It is the most explicit effort to date in the United States to stimulate states to work in a coordinated way with local school districts on statewide improvement strategies, and it includes several features that could be relevant for Brazil. Rather than channeling resources to low-performing schools, it rewards states for innovative ideas and demonstrated results—creating positive performance incentives. By stipulating the policy areas proposals must address, RTT has created a strong national push in some new policy directions, such as performance pay for teachers, standardized student assessment, alternative teacher certifcation, and charter schools. And RTT is highly selective—only 12 states of 50 are sharing the $4.35 billion pie—so the program has generated strong interest and competition for fresh ideas across all states. Box 5 describes the program in more detail. The salient point is that using federal funding to create incentives for state-municipal cooperation rather than federal-municipal relationships is a radically different paradigm that could have a profound impact on educational progress in Brazil.

Capitalize on Brazil's Education Action Lab

The long-term work of improving primary and secondary school performance is the responsibility of states and municipalities in Brazil. More than 5,500 different education systems create an incredibly rich base of program and policy experience. This report has highlighted a number of innovative and promising programs, but many, many more exist. Literally thousands of creative new education policies and programs are being tried out at this moment across Brazil by dynamic, results-oriented secretaries of education. Very few countries enjoy the scale, scope, and creativity of education policy action taking place today in Brazil, including a large number of cutting-edge policy areas in which different states and municipalities are experimenting with similar programs with slightly different design features (e.g., the teacher bonus programs in Minas Gerais, São Paulo, Pernambuco, and Rio de Janeiro municipality). The chance to study these programs systematically makes Brazil one of the world's best laboratories for generating global evidence on what works in education.

One of the most important recommendations for the federal government is to mine this rich experience more effectively. Brazil might earn an A+ in the quality of its education data and the use of data for monitoring, but it would earn a C in impact evaluation.

Impact evaluations are studies that can establish a causal link between specific programs or policies and observed results—whether improvements in student learning, student flows, and other outcomes. They are important because causal evidence forms a much stronger foundation for program design and policy choices than simple correlation of programs with outcomes. Brazil is not the only middle-income country with a limited tradition of rigorous impact evaluation in education; countries that do more, such as Mexico and Colombia, are the exception.

Awareness of the power of rigorous evaluation is spreading in developing countries, and many more evaluations are under way today than just five years ago. Global initiatives such as the Spanish Impact Evaluation Fund (SIEF) at the World Bank and the International Institute for Impact Evaluation (IIIE) are helping finance such research, recognizing that high-quality impact evaluations generate evidence and knowledge that are useful globally as well as locally. Support from both funds has helped generate the evidence on teacher incentives and ECD programs presented in this report.

Global research funding can complement, but not substitute for, national evaluation efforts. A growing number of Brazilian academics have the expertise and interest to work with states and municipalities on rigorous evaluations of their innovative programs. The most robust

> **BOX 5**
>
> ## The U.S. Race to the Top Program
>
> In February 2009, the U.S. Department of Education launched Race to the Top (RTT), a program of competitive grants awarded to states to fund innovative and ambitious reforms in public education, from kindergarten through 12th grade. The first and second phases of the program awarded a total of $4.35 billion in grants to 12 states and will affect an estimated 13.6 million students, 980,000 teachers, and 25,000 schools.
>
> RTT's goal is to encourage states to create the conditions for long-term educational improvement and student achievement, and to reward the states with the best and most viable plans. States' proposals must show plans for comprehensive education reform in four vital areas: (1) adopting standards and assessments that prepare students to succeed in college and the workplace, and to compete in the global economy; (2) building data systems that measure student growth and success, and inform teachers and principals about how they can improve instruction; (3) recruiting, developing, rewarding, and retaining effective teachers and principals, especially where they are needed most; and (4) turning around the lowest achieving schools.
>
> The plans are judged by panels of education experts on the basis of weighted criteria, which in turn are based on a system of points and priorities, including these:
> - Creating and retaining great teachers and leaders (28 percent), and ensuring their equitable distribution.
> - Identifying state success factors (25 percent), including capacity building, raising achievement, and closing gaps.
> - Developing and adopting standards and assessments (14 percent).
> - Ensuring successful conditions for high-performing charter schools (11 percent).
> - Turning around the lowest achieving schools (10 percent).
> - Implementing data systems to support instruction (9 percent).
> - Emphasizing science, technology, engineering, and math (STEM) education (3 percent).
>
> At least 50 percent of the grant must be allotted to local school districts within the state that agree to participate in the reform program; states have flexibility in how to use the balance of funding. Grants are disbursed gradually, as the winning states meet established benchmarks.
>
> During phase 1, the states of Delaware and Tennessee won grants. In August 2010, the phase 2 winners were announced: the District of Columbia, Florida, Georgia, Hawaii, Maryland, Massachusetts, New York, North Carolina, Ohio, and Rhode Island.

> **BOX 5** *continued*
>
> RTT is viewed as highly successful in achieving the federal Department of Education's core goal: to create a dynamic that encourages states to undertake difficult reforms, spreads the best reform ideas, and sets in motion new programs that will serve as models for other states to follow. Some of the reforms enacted by the first round winners are adopting common learning standards in reading and math, creating incentives to put the most effective teachers in high-need schools, and developing alternative means of teacher and principal certification. A positive externality of the competition has been that it encourages states to undertake reforms on their own to increase their chance of receiving a future RTT grant.
>
> Criticism of the program has centered on the selection process, which was to some extent subjective: a few states that have implemented well-known and highly regarded reforms did not win (Colorado and Louisiana), while others that have been ranked low on quality by national organizations in the past did win (Ohio, Maryland, New York, and Hawaii). Critics also say that the program overemphasizes momentary reform trends in education rather than long-term progress. Several teachers' unions have come out against the program as interference from the federal government.
>
> However, the media attention RTT has brought to issues of education reform and the new dynamic around federal-state relations—rewarding competitive efforts to improve rather than supporting areas of persistent failure—has led President Obama to request $1.35 billion in funding for phase 3 of the program.
>
> *Sources:* U.S. Department of Education, National Review Online, Education Week.
>
> *Contributed by Debora Brakarz*

studies are usually designed prospectively, with close collaboration between the research team and the implementing agency. This helps ensure the *sine qua non* feature of a credible evaluation: the identification of a valid comparison group.

An annual allocation as small as $20 million for competitive funding of high-caliber education impact evaluations could transform the Brazilian education research landscape. Well-designed evaluations using randomization or other technically robust methods would attract research support from global sources as well. A concerted federal strategy to support systematic research and knowledge generation from the Brazilian "education action lab" might be the single fastest road to world-class education.

References

Abadzi, H. 2009. "Instructional Time Loss in Developing Countries: Concepts, Measurement, and Implications." *World Bank Research Observer* 24(2): 267-290.
Almond, D., and J. Currie. 2011. "Human Capital Development Before Age Five." *Handbook of Labor Economics* 4(2): 1315-1486.
Alonso, M., and A Santiago. 2011. "Evidence from the Implementation of the Teach for America Model in Latin America," Inter-American Development Bank, Washington, D.C.
Arnett, J. 1989. "Caregivers in Day-Care Centers: Does Training Matter?" *Journal of Applied Developmental Psychology* 10(4): 541–52.
Autor, D., F. Levy, and R. Murnane. 2003. "The Skill Content of Recent Technological Change." *Quarterly Journal of Economics* 118(4): 1279–1333.
Ballou, D., and M. Podgursky. 2002. "Returns to Seniority Among Public School Teachers." *Journal of Human Resources* 37(4): 892–912.
Barnett, W. S., and C. R. Belfield. 2006. "Early Childhood Development and Social Mobility." *The Future of Children* 16(2): 73–98.
Barnett, W. S., and L. N. Masse. 2007. "Comparative Benefit-Cost Analysis of the Abecedarian Program and Its Policy Implications." *Economics of Education Review* 26(1): 113–25.
Barro, R. J., and J. W. Lee. 2010. "A New Data Set of Educational Attainment in the World, 1950-2010." NBER Working Paper 15902, Cambridge, MA.
Barros, R., M. Carvalho, S. Franco, R. Mendonça, and A. Rosalém. 2010. "A Short-Term Cost-Effectiveness Evaluation of Better Quality Daycare Centers." Instituto de Pesquisa Econômica Aplicada (Institute for Applied Economic Research), Rio de Janeiro.
Behrman, J., Y. Cheng, and P. Todd. 2004. "Evaluating Pre-school Programs When Length of Exposure to the Program Varies: A Nonparametric Approach." *Review of Economics and Statistics* 86(1): 108–32.

Berlinski S., S. Galiani, and P. Gertler. 2009. "The Effect of Pre-Primary Education on Primary School Performance." *Journal of Public Economics* 93: 219–34.

Birdsall, N., B. Bruns, and R. H. Sabot. 1996. "Education in Brazil: Playing a Bad Hand Badly." *In Opportunity Foregone: Education in Brazil*, ed. N. Birdsall and R. H. Sabot (p. 7–47). Washington, DC: Inter-American Development Bank.

Borko, H. 2004. "Professional Development and Teacher Learning: Mapping the Terrain." *Educational Researcher* 33(8): 3–15.

Bruns, B., T. Cruz, and E. Amorim. 2011 (forthcoming). "Inside the Classroom in Brazil: What We Can Learn from Comparative Classroom Observations." World Bank, unpublished draft.

Bruns, B., D. P. Filmer, and H. A. Patrinos. 2011. *Making Schools Work: New Evidence on Accountability Reforms*. Washington, DC: World Bank.

Campos, M. M., Y. L. Espósito, F. Rosemberg, D. F. de Andrade, S. Unbehaum, and N. Gimenes. 2010. *Educação Infantil no Brasil: Avaliação Qualitativa e Quantitativa*. São Paulo: Fundação Carlos Chagas.

Cohen, D. K., and H. Hill. 2001. *Learning Policy: When State Education Reform Works*. New Haven, CT: Yale University Press.

Danielson, C. 2007. *Enhancing Professional Practice: A Framework for Teaching*. Alexandria, VA: Association for Supervision & Curriculum Deve, 2nd edition.

Decker, P.T., D. Mayer and S. Glazerman. 2004 "The Effects of Teach for America on Students: Findings from a National Evaulation," Mathematica Policy Research. Princeton, New Jersey.

Delannoy, F., and G. Sedlacek. 2001. *Brazil—Teachers Development and Incentives: A Strategic Framework*. Washington, DC: World Bank.

de Oliveira, A. M. H. C. 2009. "An Evaluation of the Bolsa Família Program in Brazil: Expenditures, Education and Labor Outcomes." *Annals of the 2009 Annual Meeting of the Population Association of America*.

Early, D.M. et al. 2007. "Teachers' Education, Classroom Quality, and Young Children's Academic Skills: Results from Seven Studies of Preschool Programs." *Child Development* 78(2): 558–580.

Emerson, P. M., and A. Portela Souza. 2008. "Birth Order, Child Labor, and School Attendance in Brazil," *World Development* 36(9): 1647–64.

Evans, D., and K. Kosek. 2011. *Early Child Education: Making Programs Work for Brazil's Most Important Generation*. Washington, DC: World Bank. Forthcoming.

Farr, S. 2010. *Teaching as Leadership: The Highly Effective Teacher's Guide to Closing the Achievement Gap*. Hoboken, NJ: John Wiley and Sons.

Felício, F., R. T. de Menezes, and A. C. Zoghbi. 2009. "The Effects of Early Childhood Education on Literacy Scores Using Data from a New Brazilian Assessment Tool." *Annals of the 37th Brazilian Economics Meeting of the Brazilian Association of Graduate Programs in Economics (ANPEC)*, 261.

Fernandes, R. 2007. "Índice de Desenvolvimento da Educação Básica (IDEB): Metas Intermediárias para a Sua Trajetória no Brasil, Estados, Municípios e Escolas." Instituto Nacional de Estudos e Pesquisas Educacionais Anísio Teixeira (INEP), Ministério da Educação do Brasil.

Fernandes, R., and A. P. Gremaud. 2009. *Avaliação da Qualidade da Educação no Brasil*. São Paulo: Editora Moderna.

Ferraz, C., and B. Bruns. Forthcoming. "Incentives to Teach: The Effects of Performance Pay in Brazilian Schools." unpublished manuscript
Ferraz, C., and F. Finan. 2011. "Electoral Accountability and Corruption: Evidence from Audits of Local Governments" American Economic Review, 101 (June 20112):1274-1311, Rio de Janeiro, Brazil.
Filmer, D. P. 2007. "Some Lessons from School Surveys in Indonesia and Papua New Guinea." In *Are You Being Served? New Tools for Measuring Service Delivery*, ed. S. Amin, J. Das, and M. Goldstein (p. 221–232). Washington, DC: World Bank.
Garet, M., A. Porter, L. Desimone, B. Birman, and K. S. Yoon. 2001. "What Makes Professional Development Effective? Results From a National Sample of Teachers." *American Education Research Journal* 38(4): 915–45.
Glewwe, P., and A. L. Kassouf. 2008. "The Impact of the Bolsa Escola/Família Conditional Cash Transfer Program on Enrollment, Grade Promotion and Drop Out Rates in Brazil." *Annals of the 36th Brazilian Economics Meeting of the Brazilian Association of Graduate Programs in Economics (ANPEC)*, 200807211140170.
Gordon, N. and E. Vegas. 2005. "Education Finance Equalization, Spending, Teacher Quality, and Student Outcomes: The Case of Brazil's FUNDEF." In *Incentives to Improve Teaching: Lessons from Latin America*, ed. E. Vegas (p. 151–186). Washington, DC: World Bank.
Grindle, M. S. 2004. *Despite the Odds: The Contentious Politics of Education Reform*. Princeton, NJ: Princeton University Press.
Hanushek, E. A., and S. G. Rivkin. 2004. "How to Improve the Supply of High Quality Teachers." In *Brookings Papers on Education Policy*, ed. Diane Ravitch. Washington, DC: Brookings Institution.
Hanushek, E. A., and S. G. Rivkin. 2010. "Generalizations About Using Value-Added Measures of Teacher Quality." *American Economic Review* 100(2): 267–71.
Hanushek, E. A., and L. Woessmann. 2007. "The Role of Education Quality for Economic Growth." Policy Research Working Paper 4122, World Bank, Washington, DC.
Hanushek, E. A., S. G. Rivkin, and J. F. Kain. 2005. "Teachers, Schools, and Academic Achievement." *Econometrica* 73(2): 417-458.
Hanushek, E. A., J. F. Kain, D. M. O'Brien, and S. G. Rivkin. 2005. "The Market for Teacher Quality." Working Paper 11154, NBER, Washington, DC.
Harbison, R. W., and E. A. Hanushek. 1992. *Educational Performance of the Poor: Lessons from Rural Northeast Brazil*. New York: World Bank and Oxford University Press.
Heckman, J. J., S. H. Moon, R. Pinto, P. A. Savalyev, and A. Yavitz. 2010. "The Rate of Return to the HighScope Perry Preschool Program." *Journal of Public Economics* 94(1-2): 114–28.
Howes, C. H., and E. W. Smith. 1995. "Relations Among Child Care Quality, Teacher Behavior, Children's Play Activities, Emotional Security, and Cognitive Activity in Child Care." *Early Childhood Research Quarterly* 10(4): 381–404.
Instituto Nacional de Estudos e Pesquisas Educacionais Anísio Teixeira (INEP). 2010. "Na Medida: Boletim de Estudos Educacionais do INEP 2:5." Ministério da Educação, Brasília.

Lemov, D. 2010. *Teach Like a Champion: 49 Techniques That Put Students on the Path to College*. San Francisco: Jossey-Bass.

LoCasale-Crouch, J., T. Konold, R. Pianta, C. Howes, M. Burchinal, D. Bryant, R. Clifford, D. Early, and O. Barbarin. 2007. "Observed Classroom Quality Profiles in State-Funded Pre-kindergarten Programs and Associations with Teacher, Program, and Classroom Characteristics." *Early Childhood Research Quarterly* 22: 3–17.

López-Calva, L. F., and N. Lustig. 2010. "Explaining the Decline in Inequality in Latin America: Technological Change, Educational Upgrading, and Democracy." *In Declining Inequality in Latin America: A Decade of Progress?*, ed. L. F. López-Calva and N. Lustig (p. 1–24). Baltimore: Brookings Institution Press and United Nations Development Programme.

Louzano, P., V. Rocha, G.M. Moriconi, and R.P. de Oliveira. 2010. "Quem quer ser professor? Atratividade, seleção e formação docente no Brasil." *Estudos em Avaliação Educativa* 21(47): 543-568.

Magnuson, K. A., and J. Waldfogel. 2005. "Early Childhood Care and Education: Effects on Ethnic and Racial Gaps in School Readiness." *The Future of Children* 15(1): 169–96.

Menezes-Filho, N. A., and E. Pazello. 2007. "Do Teachers' Wages Matter for Proficiency? Evidence from a Funding Reform in Brazil." *Economics of Education Review* 26: 660–72.

Mendes, M. 2004. *Análise das irregularidades na administração municipal do FUNDEF: Constatações do programa de fiscalização a partir de sorteios públicos da Controladoria-Geral da União*. Transparência Brasil: São Paulo, Brazil.

Moriconi, G. 2008. "Os Professores São Mal Remunerados nas Escolas Públicas Brasileiras? Uma Análise da Atratividade da Carreira do Magistério Sob o Aspecto da Remuneração." Master's thesis presented to the Fundação Getúlio Vargas Escola de Administração de Empresas de São Paulo (EAESP-FGV).

Moss, P. 2000. "Training of Early Childhood Education and Care Staff." *International Journal of Education Research* 33: 31–53.

Nores, M., and W. S. Barnett. 2010. "Benefits of Early Childhood Interventions Across the World: (Under) Investing in the Very Young." *Economics of Education Review* 29(2): 271–82.

Odden, A., and C. Kelley. 1997. *Paying Teachers for What They Know and Do*. Thousand Oaks, CA: Corwin Press.

Organisation for Economic Co-Operation and Development (OECD). 2010. *Education at a Glance 2010: OECD Indicators*. Paris: OECD.

———. 2007. *Program for International Student Assessment (PISA) 2006— Science Competencies for Tomorrow's World, Vol. 1*. Paris: OECD.

———. 2009. *Take the Test: Sample Questions from OECD's PISA Assessments, 2000–2006*. Paris: OECD.

Paes de Barros, R., M. de Carvalho, S. Franco, and R. Mendonça. 2010. "Markets, the State, and the Dynamics of Inequality in Brazil." In *Declining Inequality in Latin America: A Decade of Progress?*, ed. L. F. López-Calva and N. Lustig (p. 134–74). Baltimore: Brookings Institution Press and United Nations Development Programme.

Paes de Barros, R., M. de Carvalho, S. Franco, R. Mendonça, and A. Rosalém. 2010. "A Short-Term Cost-Effectiveness Evaluation of Better Quality Daycare Centers." IPEA: Rio de Janeiro.

Paxson, C., and N. Schady. 2007. "Cognitive Development among Young Children in Ecuador: The Roles of Wealth, Health, and Parenting." *Journal of Human Resources* 42(1): 49-84.

Reali, A., D. Donato, J. Fogaça, L. Ortega, L. Faria, and P. Bruno. 2006. "Classe de Aceleração: Diferentes Visões de Alunos Egressos e Professores." *Annals of the 14th National Congress on Reading of the Brazilian Association on Reading (ALB), Media, Education and Reading Seminar.*

Reinikka, R., and J. Svensson. 2005. "Fighting Corruption to Improve Schooling: Evidence from a Newspaper Campaign in Uganda." *Journal of the European Economic Association* 3(2-3): 259–67.

Rodríguez, A., C. Dahlman, and J. Salmi. 2008. "Knowledge and Innovation for Competitiveness in Brazil." World Bank Institute Development Series, World Bank, Washington, DC.

Sakai, L. M., M. Whitebook, A. Wishard, and C. Howes. 2003. "Evaluating the Early Childhood Environment Rating Scale (ECERS): Assessing Differences between the First and Revised Edition." *Early Childhood Research Quarterly* 18(4): 427–45.

Schneider, A., and V. R. Ramires. 2007. *Primeira Infância Melhor: Uma Inovação em Política Pública.* Brasília: UNICEF.

Schwartzman, S. 2010. "Benchmarking Secondary Education in Brazil." Paper prepared for the International Seminar on Best Practices of Secondary Education, Inter-American Development Bank/Organization for Economic Cooperation and Development/Ministry of Education of Brazil, Brasilia. May 3-4, 2010.

Schweinhart, L. J., and D. P. Weikart. 1998. "Why Curriculum Matters in Early Childhood Education." *Educational Leadership* 55(2):57–60.

Souza, P. R. 2005. *A Revolução Gerenciada: Educação no Brasil, 1995–2002.* São Paulo: Prentice-Hall.

Stallings, J. 1985. "Instructional Time and Staff Development." In *Perspectives on Instructional Time,* ed. C. W. Fisher and D. C. Berliner (page 283-298). New York: Longman.

Tietze, W., J. Bairrão, T. B. Leal, and H. Rossbach. 1998. "Assessing Quality Characteristics of Center-Based Early Childhood Environments in Germany and Portugal: A Cross-National study." *European Journal of Psychology of Education* 13(2): 283–98.

Transparência Brasil 2005. "Brazil: The Hidden Cost of Decentralized Education." In Stealing the Future: Corruption in Classroom, edited by Bettina Meier and Michael Griffin. Berlin: Transparency International.

Umansky, I. 2005. "A Literature Review of Teacher Quality and Incentives: Theory and Evidence." In *Incentives to Improve Teaching: Lessons from Latin America,* ed. E. Vegas (p. 21–61). Washington, DC: World Bank.

Vegas, E., ed. 2005. *Incentives to Improve Teaching: Lessons from Latin America.* Washington, DC: World Bank.

Veloso, F., S. Pessôa, R. Henriques, and F. Giambiagi, eds. 2009. Educaçáo Básica no Brasil. Constiuindo o País do Futuro, Rio de Janeiro: Editora Elsevier.

Weisberg, D., S. Sexton, J. Mulhern, and D. Keeling. 2009. New York: The New Teacher Project.

Wong, L. R., and J. A. M. de Carvalho. 2006[[2004 in text]]. *"Age-Structural Transition in Brazil: Demographic Bonuses and Emerging Challenges."* In Age-Structural Transitions: Challenges for Development, ed. I. Pool, L. R. Wong, and E. Vilquin (p. 159–99). Paris: Committee for International Cooperation in National Research in Demography.

World Bank. 2001. "Brazil Early Childhood Development: A Focus on the Impact of Preschools." Human Development Department, Brazil Country Management Unit, Latin America and the Caribbean Region, World Bank, Washington, DC.

World Bank. 2002. *Constructing Knowledge Societies: New Challenges for Tertiary Education*, Directions in Development. Washington, DC: World Bank.

World Bank. 2002. "Higher Education in Brazil: Challenges and Options." Country study, World Bank, Washington, DC.

World Bank. 2008. *Looking Forward: The Challenge of Raising Education Quality in Brazil*. Washington, DC: World Bank.

World Bank. 2008. *Knowledge and Innovation for Competitiveness in Brazil*. Washington, DC. World Bank.

Annex 1.

Delivering Results for Children in Rio's Favelas: Escola Municipal Affonso Várzea

It is 7:00 a.m. at the Escola Municipal Affonso Várzea in one of Rio's most violent favelas, the Complexo do Alemão. Director Eliane Saback Sampaio stands at the school door, greeting the school's 1,100 students personally as they politely file in. Her warm smile is the first image of school for these students each day, and she routinely adds a hug, a compliment, or a message about the importance of hand-washing and eating healthy foods.

On this July day, the school is abuzz with new test results of the 2009 Index of Basic Education Development (IDEB). Affonso Várzea surpassed its target of 4.8, achieving a 5.8. Only 17 other schools in the entire 1,300-school municipal system achieved an IDEB score over 5.5. Education secretary Claudia Costin personally called Eliane to congratulate her and the school for their achievement. After 19 years as director and 23 years working at the school, Eliane is justifiably proud of the results.

Trained in mathematics, with advanced degrees in pedagogy and school administration, Eliane is an impressive figure. She believes strongly in empowering those around her; her *Prata da casa* ("specialty of the house") program gives teachers funding for special projects they develop jointly with their classes, ranging from dance and music performances to information technology training. She extends the same support to the school's lunch ladies and the *mães amigas* (mother-friends), who assist them; together they developed the project *Faça de sua alimentação uma alegria* (Make cooking fun!), in which marionettes perform little plays on how to cook different healthy foods, in the process teaching units of measure and fractions.

Eliane is passionate about her "children" and "grandchildren" at Affonso Varzea: "Our students are my children, and at this point many students in this school are the children of earlier students. You will see—if I go into any classroom and ask who are my grandchildren, many, many children will raise their hands!"

Visitors to Affonso Varzea are struck by the pristine cleanliness of the school and students' polite behavior. The walls are full of children's art, poems, and essays. The school's infrastructure is impressive—it has a dance studio, auditorium, reading room, toy room, computer lab, and 16 classrooms. There are numerous reading corners with shelves full of books, including one right at the door of the school, so that parents can easily take home books to share with their children. This was an idea of teacher Fabiana Dutra.

Thirty-five-year-old Fabiana has a degree in pedagogy from the University of Rio de Janeiro, has taught in the municipal school system since 1995, and has been at Affonso Varzea since 2006. She never considered another occupation; her mother was a teacher, and Fabiana has always been in love with books and the arts. Her house in the Engenho da Rainha neighborhood north of Rio is full of books and has poetry written on the walls. Fabiana reads compulsively (four books a week), frequently attends classical music concerts and theater, and loves to share the parks and flowers of Rio de Janeiro with her four-year-old son, Felipe. She wakes every day at 6:00 a.m. and leaves Felipe with her mother on her way to work. Fabiana has two jobs with the Rio municipal schools. In the mornings, she works as a roving master teacher of early grade reading in six different municipal schools, giving demonstration lessons and providing feedback and guidance to teachers as part of the Se Liga and Acelera programs run by the Ayrton Senna Foundation. In the afternoon, she is the librarian at Affonso Varzea. Her day officially ends at 5:30 p.m. but, like other teachers, Fabiana almost always has substantial work to do at home, planning activities for the following week. It is not unusual for her to finish at 11:00 p.m.

Fabiana is passionate about her work, but she still remembers her first years in teaching and how ill-prepared she felt. Her first assignment was in the literacy class at the Rio school CIEP Coronel Sarmiento, near the Complexo do Alemão. Expecting young children, she was shocked to find 13- and 14-year-olds in her class. "Nothing in the theory I was taught at the university prepared me for dealing with the reality of these children, who had spent years in school but still couldn't read." Only the help of other teachers, voracious outside reading on how to teach literacy, and endless experimentation enabled her, after several years, to develop effective strategies for helping all children learn to read.

Fabiana's students grow up in a world of violence and drugs. Most have never set foot outside the favela, been to a Rio beach, or even seen a shopping mall. The school is a respected island in the community and, for many students, the cleanest and safest place they know. Eliane said jokingly that many children at Affonso Varzea "want to use the bathrooms all day long," because these are the only bathrooms they have ever seen with toilets and sinks. Fabiana works hard to design reading and writing assignments that help her students articulate their fears and frustrations, develop self-esteem, and connect with the wider world. In one project, students monitored Rio's newspapers, searching for articles mentioning the Complexo do Alemão. They analyzed the tone and coverage of the articles and concluded that the favela appeared in the news only in connection with violence. Fabiana's assignment was for the students to create an alternative newspaper about their community, reporting only the positive and illustrating their articles with drawings of football games, neighborhood parties, barbeques, and street fairs. In another assignment, Fabiana asked students to choose poems that meant something to them and then write a letter to the poet. The letters were deposited in the school mailbox and opened on the first day of the school's poetry fair—helping each child make a personal connection with great literary works.

It is not easy to keep Affonso Varzea staffed with talented and committed teachers. Despite strong support from the municipal secretary and a cohesive school environment, teachers are free to request rotation to safer areas; each year, many do. But Rio's recent policies are making a difference—above all, the Escolas do Amanhã (Schools for Tomorrow) program. The 150 Rio schools that are in high-conflict areas, such as Affonso Varzea, receive special support, including infrastructure improvements, books and materials, and hardship pay for teachers. Other recent systemwide policies are also helping, such as new curriculum guideline books and materials for teachers and bimonthly student assessments. Although Affonso Varzea's team supports Rio's teacher bonus program and believes it is helping schools focus on concrete targets for improving results, they disagree with the strict policy on teacher absences. In schools that earn the bonus, teachers with five or more absences that year, whether medically excused or not, do not receive any bonus, and teachers with two to four absences have their bonuses discounted. Concerns include the incentive for teachers to work even if they are sick with communicable diseases and the chance that teachers with five or more absences will "give up" for the year, to the detriment of the school as a whole.

The city's ongoing research on the impact of the bonus program will address these issues. The teachers at Affonso Varzea are no different from those in other schools in many ways. They respond to financial incentives; they respond to nonpecuniary incentives, such as the city's public appreciation of their results; and they see their work enhanced by effective support from the central administration. But these teachers also work in some of the most difficult conditions in the world. Every day, Eliane, Fabiana, and many other teachers go above and beyond the normal work of a teacher, or any professional. Their primary motivation is the difference they make in children's lives. Fabiana points with great pride to the number of former students who have moved out of the favela and are studying at a university or working in a stable job. Eliane can see a whole generation of children in Complexo do Alemão whose lives have taken a turn for the better as a result of her work. Rio's municipal education secretary rightly calls these educators "heroes."

Contributed by Erica Amorim

Annex 2.

Delivering Results for Children in Northeast Brazil: Pernambuco Escola Estadual Tomé Francisco da Silva

It is 6:00 a.m. in Lagoa da Cruz, a small town in the Sertão desert along the border between Pernambuco and Paraíba. Ângela Maria de Oliveira, 44, wakes her nine-year-old daughter Emanuelle, and the two set off for the Tomé Francisco state school, where Ângela teaches. Miles from the nearest paved road, Ângela and Emanuelle walk to the school through dry fields, shooing chickens and cows as they go.

Every morning, Ângela teaches a class of 28 third-grade students, who are engaged and excited. According to them, she is "the coolest teacher," as she always assigns activities that incorporate games along with learning and seats the children in a circle in order to facilitate interaction. Ângela also teaches two seventh-grade history classes and a sixth-grade science class. At the end of the work day, at 6:10 p.m., she returns to her mother's house, cooks dinner for the family, helps her daughter with her homework, and finally returns to her own house to sleep.

Ângela's dedication and her students' engagement—along with that of the other teachers, students, and staff of the school—have contributed to Tomé Francisco's ascendance as a model state school. Since 2005, the school's results have consistently been well above the Pernambuco state average in all levels. In 2009, it ranked first in the state on the Index of Basic Education Development in Pernambuco (IDEPE) for grades one through four. The school achieved 100 percent of its targets under the state's pay for performance bonus during both years that the program has been in operation; thus, all personnel received the maximum salary bonus for both 2008 and 2009. Francisco Tome's principal received the state award for school management excellence; the school received a major school infrastructure award; and, in acknowledgment of the school's achievements, the governor has promised to build a road connecting Lagoa da Cruz to the capital of the municipality. The school is a source of pride for the entire community.

Most families in the vicinity of Tomé Francisco subsist on income from seasonal work on sugar cane plantations and from unemployment benefits during the off-season. Approximately 30 percent of the students receive Bolsa Família benefits; for 15 percent, these cash transfers are the only source of family income. Yet all of Tomé Francisco's students believe that doing well in school is critical for their futures, and the school reports no attendance problems. Indeed, for these children, some of the returns to education are already being seen in the short-term, with the positive attention the school has achieved throughout the state.

Nonetheless, the school has difficulty recruiting and retaining staff because of its remote location. According to the director, only people who were born there or marry a native end up staying. Staff from other areas eventually request transfers to schools closer to their own home communities or to bigger towns. Tomé Francisco is always short of cleaning, cafeteria, library, and teaching staff. Yet Ângela claims to be satisfied with her job and, with a timid smile, says, "It is no use to complain to those who are not at fault."

Funds for school inputs are scarce, but the staff of Tomé Francisco tries to manage. They buy food on the installment plan to guarantee good lunches for the students when state funds are delayed and form partnerships with other institutions to guarantee a variety of activities for the students. The teachers also contribute substantially. Ângela, for example, bought a Xerox machine for the school with her own money, as it only owned a mimeograph machine.

The school's outstanding success has created a new challenge: It is not easy to exceed its own results each year, given that they are the best in the state. To accomplish this, everyone in the school works on organizing events, sports activities, literature and music workshops, and other initiatives to spark children's love of learning.

After some years teaching the first four grades of primary school, Ângela decided to pursue a graduate degree in history at night to qualify to teach the middle grades. This routine of working during the day and studying at night is very common among the teachers in the school. Ângela becomes emotional as she remembers the difficult routine and the dangerous transportation she had to take to get to the university in the neighboring town. However, she still dreams of one day returning to school: when she retires in six years, she plans to pursue a degree in psychology.

As a child, Ângela's dream was to become a teacher. In her small town, with few job opportunities, the teaching profession is respected. The teachers and administrators of Tomé Francisco love to see their students become educators, despite what they perceive as a low financial return relative to the long hours of work.

Dedicated teachers like Ângela have a dedicated leader to rely on. The principal, Ivan José Nunes Francisco, has been leading the school for 12 years; he divides his time between his day-to-day activities and the journalists who visit every week to see this phenomenal school in the remotest part of the Sertão. Ivan believes that the main strengths of Tomé Francisco are the sense of teamwork and sharing of good teaching practices among the staff and the strong support from parents, apparent during bimonthly meetings of parents with their children's teachers. The closeness of the community is visible on signs throughout the school, in a bimonthly school newspaper, and on an Internet blog.

Ivan was elected principal of the school and believes that the democratic election of school leaders by parents and the local community was a great improvement for the system. Ângela and the other teachers in the school strongly support the new education policies of the state government. They consider the teacher bonus program a great motivator for improvement and they especially support the fact that all staff members receive the bonus, as they are all involved in the education of students. However, Ângela warns against the bonus becoming the only salary policy or the only way to motivate staff.

In this lovely school, the greatest challenge is to maintain its exceptional results. All the teachers claim to be happy with their chosen profession and are excited to see that their students are learning. With great affection, a teacher remembers advice Ângela once gave her to during a difficult time: "The teaching profession is a bitter one, but when it is carried out with love, it becomes very sweet."

Contributed by Tassia Cruz

Annex 3.

Access to and Quality of Early Childhood Development in Brazil Compared with the OECD and LAC Countries

Brazil is one of Latin America's leaders in terms of coverage in pre-primary education, behind only Mexico and Ecuador. In fact, Brazil's pre-primary education coverage even exceeds that of several OECD countries, such as the United States and the United Kingdom (see figure on p. 118). One reason for this is that Brazil has made universal access to publicly provided crèche care for its youngest children a goal, while universal public education in the United States, for example, is only provided beginning at age five. Access to both crèche care and preschools has been expanding rapidly across Brazil and is likely to continue to do so.

But the overall high rate of coverage masks massive variation across states. The maps on p. 119 show crèche and preschool access throughout Brazil. Crèche enrollment is under 10 percent in northern states and over 20 percent in southern states. Likewise, several states in the northeast and east have preschool enrollments exceeding 75 percent or even 85percent, while several in the Center-west have much lower rates of enrollment.

But access is only one piece of the story—quality is the linchpin. Some evidence from early child care programs (discussed in annex 4) suggests that if quality is not maintained, large-scale child care programs can actually be detrimental to development of some children, and in general

Figure 3.1: Gross Enrollment Ratio in Pre-Primary Education

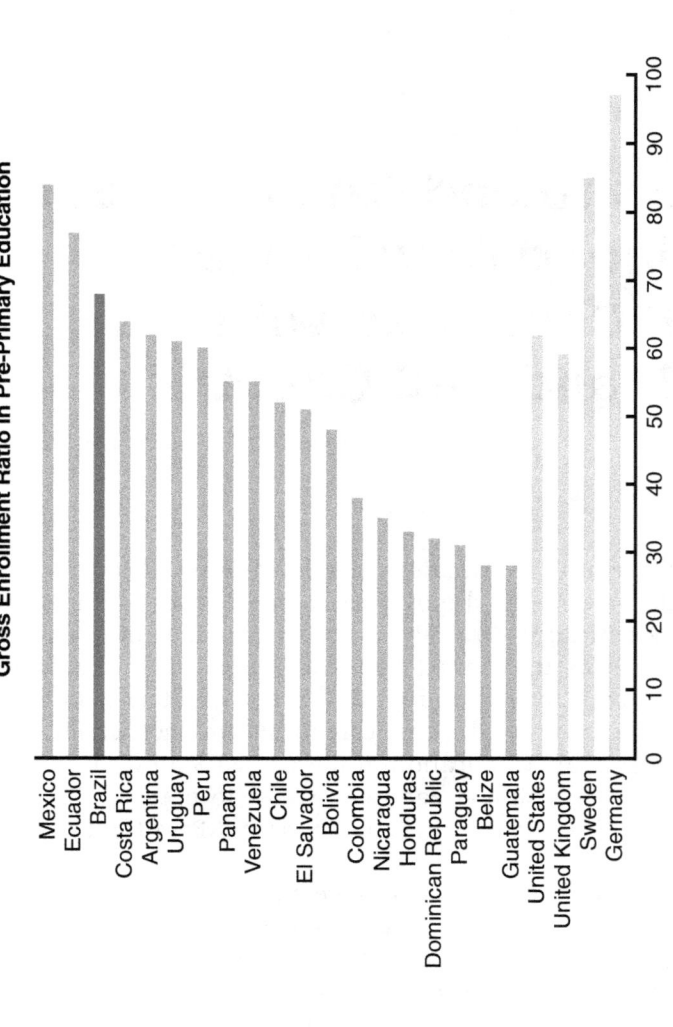

Sources: UNESCO, Strong Foundations: Early Childhood Care and Education. EFA Global Monitoring Report 2007, 2006, appendix table 12.

Annex 3 | **119**

Figure 3.2: ECE coverage by state, 2009

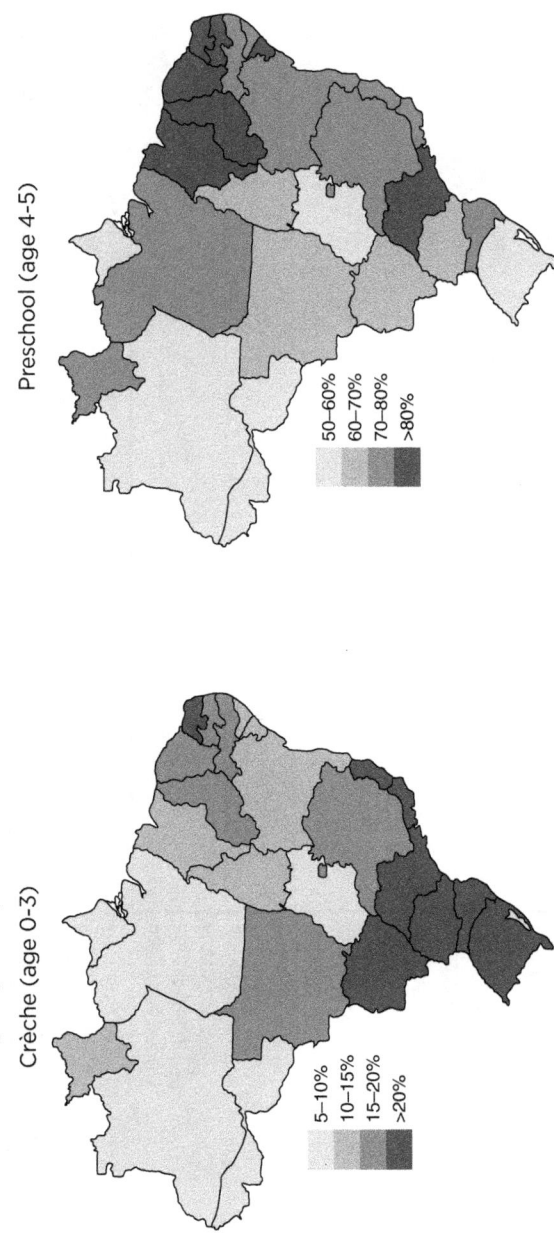

Source: Evans D, and K Kosec, "Early Child Education: Making Programs Work for Brazil's Most Important Generation," World Bank, 2011.

Figure 3.3: Pupil-Teacher Ratio in Pre-primary Education, 2004

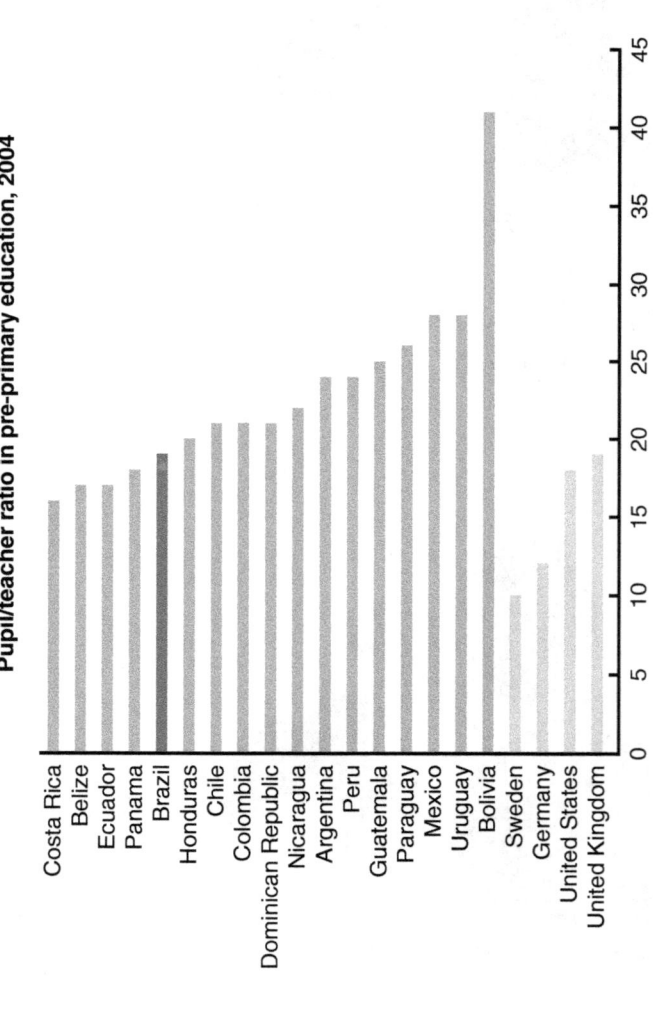

Sources: UNESCO, Strong Foundations: Early Childhood Care and Education. EFA Global Monitoring Report 2007, 2006, appendix table 10A.

can fail to deliver the desired high returns. International indicators of quality in pre-primary education are limited. On one indicator—pupil-teacher ratio—Brazil compares well, with a relatively low number of pupils per teacher. But it is not the Latin American leader.

A recent study in six state capitals around Brazil (Belém, Campo Grande, Florianópolis, Fortaleza, Rio de Janeiro, and Teresina) carefully examined the quality of pre-primary institutions in 18 to 30 institutions per state on a broad range of characteristics, including personal care, activities, interaction, space and equipment, program structure, teaching speaking and comprehension, and faculty and parent involvement (Campos et al. 2010.) Overall, 50 percent of crèches surveyed were rated "inadequate" on a standardized international scale, 37 percent were rated "basic," 12 percent were rated "adequate," and only 1 percent were rated "good."[16] Quality was slightly better at the preschool level, with respective ratings of 30 percent, 42 percent, 24 percent, and 4 percent. These ratings leave much room for improvement. At both levels of education, the weakest areas were activities for the children (e.g., blocks for play, music and movement activities, activities that demonstrate nature and science principles) and program structure. Interactions between staff and children rated high. The combination of strong interactions and weak activities suggest that staff desire to engage with the children but lack the skills to effectively stimulate their cognitive and social development.

---

16 For crèches, the instrument used was the Infant/Toddler Environment Rating Scale, Revised Edition (ITERS-R); for preschools, the Early Childhood Environment Rating Scale, Revised Edition (ECERS-R).

Annex 4.

Global Evidence on Universal Versus Targeted Early Childhood Development Coverage

The best evidence regarding the effectiveness of early childhood education comes from high-quality programs targeted toward vulnerable children in the United States. Both the Perry Preschool Program (which provided preschool and home visits for children ages three to five) and the Abecedarian program (which provided full-day preschool to children beginning at four months of age) led to major improvements in short- and long-term education performance, including finishing high school on time and completing university study, in addition to a range of broader life impacts, such as lower unemployment and fewer arrests at age 40 (Barnett 2009).

These were both small programs, targeting fewer than 150 needy children each. The Head Start program in the United States targets low-income children with preschool for three-, four-, and five-year-olds; it reaches approximately 800,000 children each year. Several evaluations, including a randomized trial, have suggested that Head Start has positive effects on cognitive ability (especially language ability) and grade progression, and there is evidence that the program reduces crime and other behavior problems (Almond and Currie 2011).

The evidence is mixed for larger scale, less-targeted programs, which is where Brazil's current crèche and preschool policy would lead (see table 4.1). Some evaluations have found evidence of positive educational and behavioral outcomes (e.g., Argentina and Norway), while others have found negative behavioral outcomes (e.g., Quebec). There is a great deal of variation among programs and outcomes, and clearly the impact will depend on the quality and intensiveness of the program relative to what children would receive at home.

In Brazil, data on the impact of crèches and preschools is limited. Early research found a positive correlation between preschool attendance and both education attainment and earnings, but the study looked at people who attended preschool between 1937 and 1976, and the methodology essentially involved comparing people who seem similar except for whether or not they attended preschool (World Bank 2001). This kind of comparison is challenging, as families that invest in preschool may also invest in other opportunities for their children that are not captured in the analysis. A recent study by Fundação Carlos Chagas compared the performance on the Provinha Brasil of children who attended preschools with the performance of those who did not in three cities (Campo Grande, Florianópolis, and Teresina) and found that early childhood education explained about half of differences between students on the Provinha, but that these impacts are concentrated on children who attended higher quality preschools. A rigorous evaluation of Rio de Janeiro's crèches is taking advantage of a lottery that assigned children to crèches in order to compare truly comparable children who had access to public daycare and who did not. Results are expected at the end of 2011.

Table 4.1. Impact Evaluation Evidence on Universal Early Childhood Education Programs

Site studied	Program evaluated	Results
Argentina[25]	Expansion of preschool (ages 3-5)	• Improvement in third-grade test scores
		• Improvement in self-control (attention, effort, class participation, and discipline)
Denmark[26]	Center-based care (age 3) compared with informal family day care (a person in the community provides care in her home) compared with parental care	• No cognitive or behavioral differences at age 11
Norway[27]	Expansion of government provided child care (ages 3-6)	• At age 30, positive effects on educational attainment and labor market attachment
		• Reduced welfare dependency
Quebec (Canada)[28]	Expansion of day care (infancy-4 years) in 1990s	• Adverse effects on child anxiety, aggressiveness, and motor skills
		• Adverse effects on chance of a child being in excellent health
USA[29]	Expansion of kindergarten (age 5)	• Improved high school completion for white children
		• No benefits for black children (probably because universal kindergarten crowded out more targeted programs)

---

17   S. Berlinski, S. Galiani, and P. Gertler, "The Effect of Pre-primary Education on Primary School Performance," *Journal of Public Economics* 93 (2009): 219–34.
18   N. Gupta and M. Simonsen, "Effects of Universal Child Care Participation on Pre-teen Skills and Risky Behaviours," European Association of Labor Economists Working Paper, 2010.
19   T. Havnes and M. Mogstad, "No Child Left Behind Universal Child Care and Children's Long-Run Outcomes," Statistics Norway Discussion Paper 582, May 2009. http://www.uis.no/getfile.php/SV/Magne%20Mogstad.pdf.
20   M. Baker, J. Gruber, and K. Milligan, "Universal Childcare, Maternal Labor Supply and Family Well-Being," *Journal of Political Economy* 116(4) (2008): 709–45.
21   E. Cascio, "Do Investments in Universal Early Education Pay Off? Long-Term Effects of Introducing Kindergartens into Public Schools," NBER Working Paper 14951, May 2009.

Annex 5.

Skills Composition in the Brazilian Labor Market

We analyzed changes in skills composition in the Brazilian labor market following the methodology used by Murnane and colleagues to explain changes in the supply and demand for different labor skills in the U.S. labor market over the 1980–2008 period. The essence of this method is to decompose different occupations into the underlying types of skills they require. Analyzing changes in occupations alone might not appropriately signal the skills and abilities required in a context of rapid educational expansion and limited quality.

Our first step was to use an occupational classification scheme to identify and estimate the importance of each skill for the most important occupations in the labor market. The initial intention was to base our analysis on a scheme for Brazil, but such information is not available for Brazil. Thus, we looked for an alternative source of such detailed information.

We found that the Occupational Network Database (ONET), although not a perfect match, is an appropriate reference scheme. ONET provides detailed information on the importance of different skills and tasks in every occupation. Because such information is reported by peers or people who are familiar with the occupation, we believe it accurately reflects how important each skill is for adequate performance in a given occupation. This dataset provides the percentage distribution of the importance of each set of skills, measured on a 5-point scale. It also provides aggregated information on the average score on the same scale. We used the latter for our analysis.

In operational terms, we used a series of datasets corresponding to Brazil's National Household Survey (Perquisa Nacional por Amostragem de Domicílios, PNAD). In each dataset, we identified the occupation reported by every person; eventually, we could map them to the occupations in ONET. An initial limitation was that PNAD used at least three different occupational classification schemes during the period 1980–2000, so we had to find each one's respective equivalence. To tackle this, we used equivalence tables available from different sources. We were able to map most of the occupations to the International Standard Classification of Occupations version 1988 (ISCO-88) developed by the International Labor Organization (ILO). To make it compatible with ONET, we aggregated the occupations in the ONET database to the U.S. Bureau of Labor Standard Occupational Classification (SOC) System in its 2000 version, then mapped it to the ISCO-88 scheme using the Gazenboom and Treiman standardization routines. This approach proved to be more satisfactory in terms of coverage than the initial mapping we did based on the 70 occupations in the Brazilian labor market, identified for every decade, which represented around 80 percent of the working population. In both cases, however, we could not assign skills to some occupations that exist in the ONET dataset and we encountered other occupations that have not been established in the ONET dataset. Usually this occurs with occupations in the lowest rungs of the occupational ladder. Given Brazil's occupational structure, a lack of information for lower-level occupations that account for a significant part of the labor force biases the scores upward (ie, workers in subsistence agriculture, for example, represent approximately 9 percent of Brazil's total labor force.)

The equivalence table allowed us to match occupations with scores for the importance of each of the core skills they require. We built a set of composite measures of the skills identified by Acemoglu and Autor, using the ONET dataset. We ended up with a set of five composite measures or group tasks comprising 16 specific tasks. Specific tasks that make up each aggregated measures are shown in table 5.1.

Composite Scores by Income

Table 5.2 shows the average score for each of the composite task measures disaggregated by income quintiles for selected years in different periods. Scores are expressed in the original 5-point scale. In general, we observed an increase in the average importance of the cognitive-related tasks in every period. Manual task scores tended to lose importance during the 1980s but remained relatively stable in the 2000s.

Table 5.1. Core Labor Force Skills and Underlying Abilities

Grouped Task	Specific Task
Nonroutine cognitive: analytical	Analyzing data/information
	Thinking creatively
	Interpreting information for others
Nonroutine cognitive: interpersonal	Establishing and maintaining personal relationships
	Guiding, directing, and motivating subordinates
	Coaching/developing others
Routine cognitive	Importance of repeating the same tasks
	Importance of being exact or accurate
	Structured versus unstructured work (reverse)
Routine manual	Pace determined by speed of equipment
	Controlling machines and processes
	Making repetitive motions
Nonroutine manual/physical	Operating vehicles, mechanized devices, or equipment
	Using hands to handle, control, or feel objects, tools, or controls
	Manual dexterity
	Spatial orientation

Sources: Acemoglu and Autor (2010).

As expected, persons in the lowest income quintiles tend to score higher in routine-manual occupations, while those in higher quintiles are more heavily engaged in occupations requiring nonroutine cognitive tasks. This suggests that the labor market rewards highly specialized skills.

Changes in Specific Task Requirements

A plausible explanation for the lack of change in the skills distribution might be the slow pace of change in skills distribution in spite of changes in the proportion of people working in various occupations. To illustrate this point, we estimated the importance of every task in occupations

Table 5.2. Average Composite Task Scores by Income Quintiles in Brazil, Selected Years

Income quintile	Nonroutine cognitive: analytical	Nonroutine cognitive: interpersonal	Routine cognitive	Routine manual	Nonroutine manual/ physical
1981					
Q 1	2.543	2.819	2.839	2.838	2.724
Q 2	2.651	2.844	2.923	2.818	2.762
Q 3	2.706	2.864	2.989	2.746	2.697
Q 4	2.820	2.924	3.045	2.632	2.576
Q 5	3.126	3.124	3.039	2.374	2.245
Total	2.757	2.909	2.961	2.692	2.610
1989					
Q 1	2.549	2.828	2.837	2.787	2.684
Q 2	2.605	2.819	2.972	2.766	2.650
Q 3	2.697	2.872	2.998	2.691	2.607
Q 4	2.833	2.953	3.023	2.588	2.509
Q 5	3.111	3.156	3.012	2.350	2.222
Total	2.755	2.924	2.964	2.639	2.537
1992					
Q 1	2.568	2.839	2.831	2.795	2.699
Q 2	2.579	2.821	2.937	2.769	2.648
Q 3	2.673	2.865	2.993	2.695	2.596
Q 4	2.826	2.959	3.028	2.574	2.480
Q 5	3.137	3.152	3.059	2.390	2.229
Total	2.752	2.925	2.966	2.648	2.535
1998					
Q 1	2.565	2.832	2.844	2.779	2.702
Q 2	2.573	2.827	2.939	2.735	2.622
Q 3	2.663	2.870	3.008	2.678	2.564
Q 4	2.810	2.969	3.026	2.568	2.468
Q 5	3.184	3.212	3.032	2.340	2.189
Total	2.757	2.941	2.968	2.622	2.511

Income quintile	Nonroutine cognitive: analytical	Nonroutine cognitive: interpersonal	Routine cognitive	Routine manual	Nonroutine manual/ physical
2002					
Q1	2.521	2.814	2.862	2.697	2.612
Q2	2.549	2.818	2.987	2.727	2.586
Q3	2.647	2.861	3.044	2.699	2.580
Q4	2.829	2.967	3.063	2.587	2.530
Q5	3.235	3.244	3.019	2.291	2.195
Total	2.762	2.944	2.997	2.597	2.497
2008					
Q1	2.540	2.822	2.898	2.681	2.600
Q2	2.552	2.805	3.031	2.721	2.554
Q3	2.659	2.859	3.064	2.684	2.562
Q4	2.849	2.969	3.078	2.588	2.514
Q5	3.262	3.254	3.022	2.296	2.199
Total	2.780	2.946	3.022	2.591	2.484

Sources: PNAD for selected years, elaboration by authors.

Note: Task scores were estimated using the ONET database and following procedures detailed in Acemoglu and Autor (2010). Scored on a 5-point scale: 1 is less important and 5 is more important.

for selected years. In table 5.3 we show the percentage of occupations that considered each task important on 5-point scale. In most cases, the relative importance of underlying tasks within each major skill category has remained stable over almost 30 years. There are some exceptions, but they are not enough to create an overall change.

For the sake of comparison with a more mature economy, we estimated a similar table for the United States using the American Community Survey for the years 2006–2008. We restricted the population to native-born Americans to eliminate a possible immigration effect. As expected, we observed differences between the two countries.

Finally, we combined the nonroutine or high-level analytical, interpersonal, and manual skills that Autor and colleagues called "new economy skills" into a single variable and compared this with routine cognitive skills and routine manual skills (table 5.4).

Table 5.3. Importance of Specific Skills (by percentage)

Group Task	Specific Task	1981	1989	1992	1999	2002	2008	U.S. Native Born (ACS, 2006-2008)
Nonroutine cognitive: analytical	Analyzing data/information	2%	2%	2%	3%	3%	4%	10%
	Thinking creatively	5%	6%	5%	6%	7%	7%	12%
	Interpreting information for others	2%	2%	2%	2%	3%	3%	6%
Nonroutine cognitive: interpersonal	Establishing and maintaining personal relationships	5%	6%	5%	6%	14%	14%	29%
	Guiding, directing, and motivating subordinates	2%	4%	3%	4%	1%	1%	6%
	Coaching/developing others	1%	1%	2%	2%	3%	4%	8%
Routine cognitive	Importance of being exact or accurate	35%	38%	33%	34%	42%	45%	61%
	Importance of repeating the same tasks	9%	9%	8%	8%	8%	9%	16%
	Structured versus unstructured work (reverse)	53%	51%	53%	51%	42%	41%	51%
Routine manual	Controlling machines and processes	4%	4%	4%	3%	5%	5%	4%
	Making repetitive motions	11%	11%	11%	12%	16%	15%	14%
	Pace determined by speed of equipment	2%	2%	2%	2%	3%	3%	1%
	Spatial orientation	0%	0%	0%	0%	0%	0%	1%
Nonroutine manual/physical	Manual dexterity	1%	1%	0%	0%	1%	1%	1%
	Operating vehicles, mechanized devices, or equipment	1%	1%	1%	1%	6%	5%	6%
	Using hands to handle, control, or feel objects, tools, or controls	23%	23%	21%	21%	25%	26%	18%

Source: Authors' estimates.

Note: Each figure indicates the percentage of occupations in which the skill is considered important or very important for adequate performance in that occupation, out of the total number of occupations in every year.

Table 5.4. Trends in Skills Distribution in Brazil and the United States, 1980–2009

		New Economy	Routine Cognitive Skills	Routine Manual Skills
United States	1980	50%	50%	50%
United States	2008	55%	47%	47%
Brazil	1981	48%	30%	58%
Brazil	1986	47%	31%	57%
Brazil	1992	48%	29%	57%
Brazil	1997	48%	30%	56%
Brazil	2002	47%	37%	56%
Brazil	2005	47%	39%	55%
Brazil	2009	48%	40%	54%

Sources: United States: 5 percent sample of 1980 U.S. Census and 2006–2008 American Community Survey. Brazil: PNAD, various years between 1981 and 2009.

Note: The figures in this table show the changes in skills distribution using as a reference point the percentile distribution of the skills in the United States in 1980. The mean percentile is set at 50 for 1980, and the other figures are calculated using that distribution.

Annex 6.

Tables

Table 6.1. Public Investment in Education Per Student, 2000-2008 (Rs, nominal prices)

	Total (all levels)	Basic Education	ECD	Tertiary Education		Secondary Education	Tertiary Education
				Early years	Late years		
2000	970	808	924	794	811	770	8,927
2001	1,082	902	898	845	951	944	9,500
2002	1,214	1,005	952	1,111	1,032	747	10,135
2003	1,329	1,116	1,197	1,176	1,117	938	9,706
2004	1,513	1,284	1,372	1,359	1,374	939	10,573
2005	1,7	1,44	1,373	1,607	1,53	1,004	11,363
2006	2,042	1,773	1,533	1,825	2,004	1,417	11,820
2007	2,467	2,163	1,954	2,274	2,369	1,735	13,089
2008	2,995	2,632	2,206	2,761	2,946	2,122	14,763

Source: INEP/MEC.

6.2. Public Investment in Education Per Student, 2000–2008 (2008 constant Rs)

	Total (all levels)	Basic Education	ECD	Elementary Education		Secondary Education	Tertiary Education
				Early years	Late years		
2000	1,667	1,388	1,587	1,365	1,393	1,324	15,341
2001	1,726	1,439	1,433	1,349	1,518	1,506	15,161
2002	1,722	1,426	1,35	1,576	1,463	1,06	14,374
2003	1,724	1,448	1,553	1,526	1,45	1,217	12,594
2004	1,824	1,548	1,655	1,638	1,656	1,133	12,749
2005	1,94	1,643	1,566	1,833	1,746	1,146	12,965
2006	2,259	1,961	1,695	2,019	2,217	1,568	13,076
2007	2,612	2,291	2,069	2,408	2,509	1,837	13,861
2008	2,995	2,632	2,206	2,761	2,946	2,122	14,763

Source: INEP/MEC.

Table 6.3. Public Spending per Student in Primary Education, by Region and State, selected years, 1994-2007 (in 2007 constant Rs)

	1994	1998	2002		2006		2007	
			Early Years	Late years	Early Years	Late years	Early Years	Late years
Brazil	423.6	1,372.2	1,644.5	1,527.1	1,932.1	2,121.5	2,273.5	2,368.7
North	275.8	1,158.0						
Rondônia	219.6	1,227.6	1,504.4	1,561.1	1,915.5	1,939.6	2,217.2	2,118.8
Acre	505.3	1,969.7	1,903.5	2,333.5	2,674.6	2,859.1	3,055.7	3,467.4
Amazonas	301.9	1,249.4	935.3	1,334.0	1,439.7	1,747.9	1,606.7	1,796.9
Roraima	439.8	2,120.5	2,855.9	3,415.0	3,267.2	3,410.5	3,915.9	4,194.3
Pará	235.4	979.7	781.3	1,125.8	963.3	1,030.0	1,503.8	1,453.5
Amapá	447.6	1,439.4	2,225.6	2,281.6	2,553.3	2,681.4	2,649.9	2,764.1
Tocantins	278.3	1,077.3	1,347.7	1,468.5	1,922.3	2,016.2	2,164.6	2,284.6

Sources: IPEA/DISOC, IBGE/MP & INEP/MEC.

Annex 6 | 139

	1994	1998	2002		2006		2007	
			Early Years	Late years	Early Years	Late years	Early Years	Late years
Northeast	235.7	954.9						
Maranhão	180.0	822.9	748.8	1,047.3	883.3	1,053.8	1,532.8	1,463.8
Piauí	235.3	923.3	962.0	1,182.4	1,286.8	1,373.2	1,345.2	1,456.3
Ceará	259.8	1,013.6	845.3	1,118.7	994.6	1,477.5	1,483.6	2,318.6
Rio Grande do Norte	261.8	1,354.5	1,204.2	1,567.5	1,708.0	1,837.7	1,947.2	2,057.4
Paraíba	250.6	901.2	1,004.7	1,213.0	1,227.6	1,429.9	1,541.2	1,633.1
Pernambuco	172.0	922.8	1,155.7	910.3	1,206.9	1,379.2	1,466.7	1,672.3
Alagoas	228.0	983.5	839.6	944.8	1,018.9	1,275.6	1,457.1	1,656.9
Sergipe	339.6	1,086.8	1,170.6	1,309.8	1,605.6	1,652.2	1,844.6	1,845.8
Bahia	255.6	924.0	938.5	1,167.9	1,111.8	1,379.9	1,500.8	1,646.4
Southeast	520.5	1,643.7						
Minas Gerais	398.9	1,535.2	1,555.5	1,591.8	1,817.4	1,815.5	2,007.2	1,885.0
Espírito Santo	518.6	1,777.6	1,574.2	1,321.0	2,406.1	2,608.4	2,691.8	2,764.7
Rio de Janeiro	597.6	1,800.4	1,949.3	2,171.9	2,909.9	3,866.3	3,024.9	3,941.7
São Paulo	573.0	1,644.0	2,856.4	1,949.1	3,344.1	3,283.6	3,671.3	3,432.7

Sources: IPEA/DISOC, IBGE/MP & INEP/MEC.

	1994	1998	2002		2006		2007	
			Early Years	Late years	Early Years	Late years	Early Years	Late years
South	515.9	1,541.2						
Paraná	480.9	1,576.6	1,859.6	1,836.6	2,190.2	1,957.4	2,280.3	2,833.3
Santa Catarina	498.9	1,267.6	1,799.0	1,505.3	1,964.1	2,055.0	1,915.4	1,864.3
Rio Grande do Sul	562.8	1,661.6	1,794.5	1,534.2	2,385.1	2,198.5	2,337.5	2,143.8
Center West	381.8	1,722.8						
Mato Grosso do Sul	381.5	1,506.6	1,517.8	1,528.6	2,180.0	2,200.8	2,706.9	2,763.9
Mato Grosso do Sul	305.5	1,392.9	2,289.4	1,437.4	2,263.2	1,997.6	2,541.8	2,284.7
Goiás	191.1	907.9	1,774.3	1,286.2	2,001.7	1,982.0	2,235.6	2,173.6
Distrito Federal	1,034.2	4,576.2	3,686.6	4,453.3	3,222.8	2,960.0	3,272.3	3,194.0

Sources: IPEA/DISOC, IBGE/MP & INEP/MEC.

Figure 6.1. State and Municipal Expenditures per Student in Basic Education, Disaggregated by Region, 2004-2008 (2008 Rs)

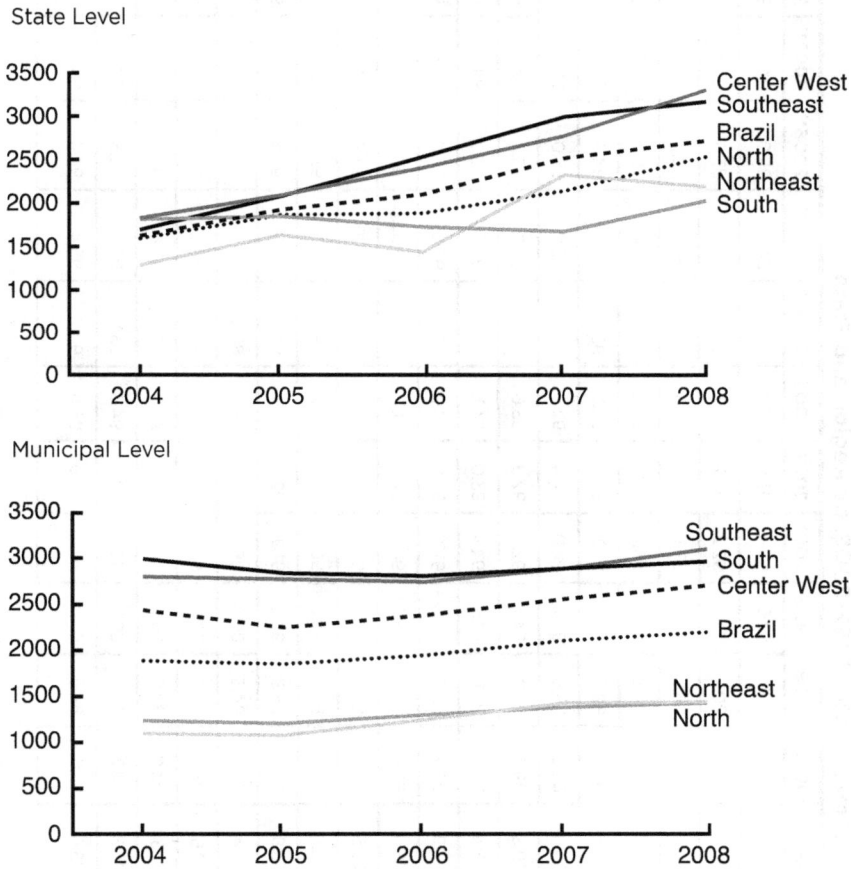

Sources: Brazilian financial data and school censuses of various years, elaborated by authors.

Table 6.4. Primary Education Net Enrollment Ratio, 1992-2008, by Region and State

	1992	1993	1995	1996	1997	1998	1999	2001	2002	2003	2004[*1]	2005[*1]	2006[*1]	2007[*1]	2008[*1]
Brazil	81.4	83.0	85.5	86.6	88.6	91.0	92.5	93.4	93.9	94.0	94.0	94.6	95.0	94.6	94.9
North	82.6	83.7	86.3	86.5	86.8	90.1	91.6	92.2	92.2	92.8	92.2	93.2	93.9	93.3	93.6
Acre	88.4	85.0	89.9	89.9	88.7	86.5	88.8	93.1	93.9	95.3	90.7	91.0	92.7	88.8	92.2
Amapá	93.8	86.9	90.2	92.7	90.2	94.8	95.6	96.1	91.8	94.5	94.4	95.8	95.6	93.5	94.6
Amazonas	82.8	81.7	84.9	85.7	84.0	89.2	91.1	91.9	92.1	91.8	93.9	94.8	94.9	94.1	94.4
Pará	82.3	84.6	84.9	85.6	86.5	88.8	91.0	92.0	92.4	92.5	91.1	92.0	93.0	92.9	93.0
Rondônia	87.7	87.9	90.2	89.3	89.3	93.2	94.7	92.7	92.9	93.6	92.8	93.8	93.7	92.7	93.3
Roraima	95.4	95.4	96.9	95.4	89.6	93.1	97.5	94.4	83.0	94.1	95.5	95.5	95.0	94.2	93.3
Tocantins	73.2	78.2	85.7	83.9	88.2	92.3	90.3	91.7	92.6	93.2	92.5	93.8	95.3	95.6	95.9
Northeast	69.7	72.7	76.1	78.0	81.9	86.7	89.2	90.7	91.6	91.7	91.7	92.5	93.6	93.7	94.3
Alagoas	64.8	69.5	67.6	70.5	77.1	81.0	84.7	90.6	91.4	89.7	91.3	94.2	92.7	93.6	93.6
Bahia	69.0	70.9	75.8	80.0	81.7	85.5	90.0	90.5	91.3	91.6	89.9	91.9	93.5	93.6	94.0
Ceará	66.4	67.6	71.0	75.8	83.9	88.8	90.6	91.9	92.6	91.9	93.7	92.9	94.6	94.8	95.0
Maranhão	63.8	70.5	72.7	72.4	75.9	84.5	85.0	86.6	88.1	86.5	88.8	88.7	91.7	91.8	94.1
Paraíba	69.4	73.0	77.4	77.6	83.3	88.2	92.5	93.2	93.2	95.4	94.1	93.6	93.8	93.8	95.9
Pernambuco	75.6	77.4	80.8	81.5	83.0	88.0	89.1	90.0	92.5	92.6	92.8	93.6	93.3	93.9	93.0
Piauí	71.2	78.2	79.4	76.8	82.7	87.8	89.1	93.1	92.7	94.3	93.1	93.1	95.3	94.2	94.9
Rio Grande do Norte	78.5	79.2	85.5	85.6	87.6	89.6	93.0	93.5	93.9	95.6	94.7	95.4	94.4	95.3	96.1

Source: (PNAD).

	1992	1993	1995	1996	1997	1998	1999	2001	2002	2003	2004*1	2005*1	2006*1	2007*1	2008*1
Sergipe	77.9	81.0	83.9	82.9	87.0	90.0	90.5	91.2	91.4	94.1	92.2	93.6	94.8	93.1	95.3
Center-West	85.9	85.6	88.1	89.8	90.5	93.1	93.6	94.7	93.9	94.0	94.5	94.9	95.5	94.8	94.5
Distrito Federal	92.2	92.6	92.9	93.9	94.8	95.5	94.8	95.2	93.6	93.7	95.6	94.7	94.5	94.9	95.9
Goiás	83.3	83.2	85.9	88.5	89.7	91.8	93.9	94.4	94.2	94.4	94.1	94.9	95.9	95.4	94.3
Mato Grosso do Sul	87.2	84.7	87.6	90.3	89.9	92.9	93.3	95.4	95.0	96.1	96.4	95.9	96.2	95.5	95.6
Mato Grosso	85.0	85.4	89.2	88.9	89.3	94.2	92.2	94.1	92.6	91.9	92.8	94.1	94.9	92.9	92.8
Southeast	88.1	89.2	91.0	91.2	92.3	93.2	94.2	94.8	95.2	95.3	95.5	96.0	95.8	95.4	95.7
Espírito Santo	87.7	83.1	87.2	89.4	91.6	91.1	93.2	93.5	94.0	94.9	95.1	92.9	95.5	94.0	96.0
Minas Gerais	84.0	85.3	88.6	89.4	91.9	92.8	94.3	94.9	95.7	96.0	96.0	96.0	94.7	94.9	95.5
Rio de Janeiro	85.8	87.9	89.3	88.6	88.7	90.2	92.1	91.4	92.3	92.6	92.3	93.8	93.7	94.0	93.5
São Paulo	91.1	92.3	93.3	93.3	93.9	94.8	94.9	96.1	96.1	96.0	96.4	97.0	97.2	96.3	96.6
South	86.9	88.6	90.3	92.2	93.3	94.2	95.2	95.5	95.9	95.8	95.6	96.1	96.2	95.3	95.2
Paraná	85.3	86.2	89.3	90.9	92.6	93.9	94.0	95.2	96.2	95.2	95.4	95.8	95.8	94.2	95.2
Rio Grande do Sul	88.7	90.6	91.0	92.9	93.7	94.5	95.6	95.0	95.4	95.8	95.4	96.0	96.1	95.5	95.7
Santa Catarina	86.6	89.4	91.1	93.3	93.8	94.3	96.4	96.8	96.4	97.3	96.5	96.9	97.3	96.8	94.4

Source: (PNAD).

Table 6.5. FUNDEB-Mandated Public Spending Per Student by Educational Level, 2009

	Coefficient	National minimum	Rs/student
Early Childhood Education		1350.09	
Crèche			
Public - full time	1.1		1485
Public - part time	0.8		1080
Conveniada - full time	0.95		1283
Conveniada - part time	0.8		1080
Preschool			
Full time	1.15		1553
Part time	0.9		1215
Elementary Education			
Early years (urban areas)	1		1350
Early years (rural areas)	1.05		1418
Late years (urban areas)	1.1		1486
Late years (rural areas)	1.15		1553
Full-time education	1.25		1688
Secondary Education			
Urban	1.2		1620
Rural	1.25		1688
Full-time education	1.3		1755
Integrated technical/vocational education	1.3		1755
Special Education	1.2		1620
Indigenous Education and Quilombolas	1.2		1620
Adult and Youth Education			
With process evaluation	0.7		945
Integrated technical/vocational education	0.7		945

Source: MEC.

Table 6.6. Public Expenditures in Education by Government Level, 2000/2009 (billions of 2009 Rs)

	Municipalities	States	Federal	Total
2009	62	71	37	169
2008	57	70	26	153
2007	53	61	24	138
2006	42	58	21	121
2005	37	54	20	112
2004	37	53	20	109
2003	41	57	21	118
2002	33	39	22	94
2001	35	60	22	117
2000	35	56	21	112
1998	35	53	34	122
1996	52	45	25	121

Source: Brazilian National Treasury.

Figure 6.2. Evolution of Secondary Enrollments, in Public and Private Institutions

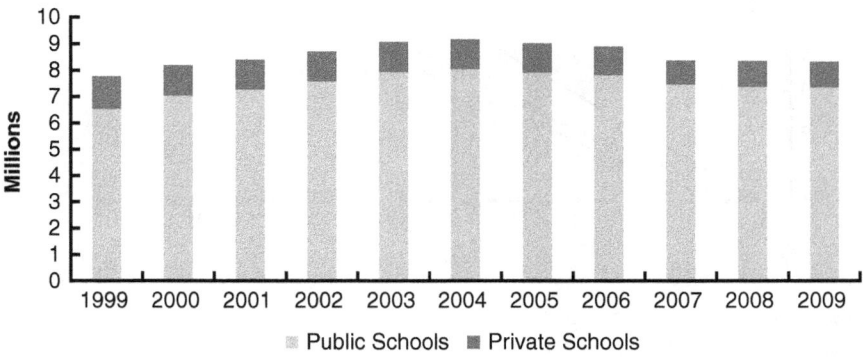

Source: INEP/MEC.

Figure 6.3. Evolution of Secondary Enrollment by School Shift

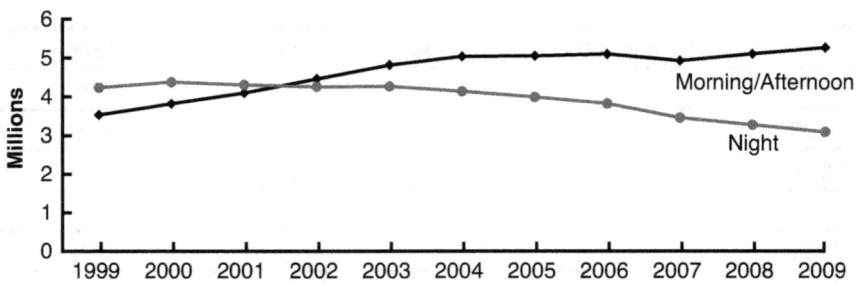

Source: INEP/MEC.

Figure 6.4. Grade Attainment of Enrolled Students by Age

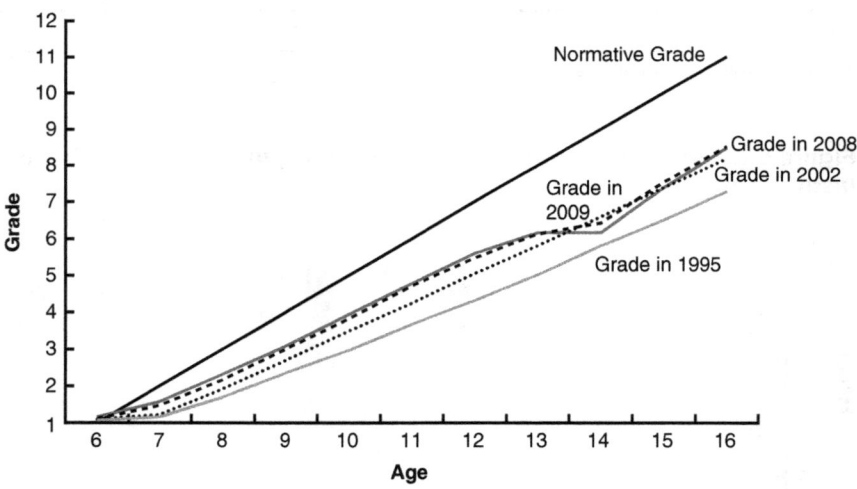

Sources: PNAD (1995, 2002, 2008, 2009).
Note: For individuals between 6 and 16 years old who are currently enrolled in school.

Table 6.7. Secondary Enrollments in State Schools: Share of Enrollments in Night Shifts and Index of Basic Education Development (IDEB), 2005, 2007, and 2009

State	Enrollment in Night Shift (%)				IDEB 2005	IDEB 2007	IDEB 2009
	2005	2007	2009	Diff.			
Tocantins	61	52	36	-25	2.9	3.1	3.3
Distrito Federal	32	27	17	-15	3.0	3.2	3.2
Paraíba	50	42	35	-14	2.6	2.9	3.0
Minas Gerais	52	46	39	-13	3.4	3.5	3.6
Mato Grosso	54	45	41	-13	2.6	3.0	2.9
Mato Grosso do Sul	50	44	38	-12	2.8	3.4	3.5
Alagoas	60	55	49	-11	2.8	2.6	2.8
Pará	57	49	46	-11	2.6	2.3	3.0
Rondônia	45	39	34	-11	3.0	3.1	3.7
Acre	35	28	24	-11	3.0	3.3	3.5
Piauí	67	61	57	-10	2.3	2.5	2.7
Rio de Janeiro	51	47	41	-10	2.8	2.8	2.8
Santa Catarina	50	45	40	-10	3.5	3.8	3.7
Espírito Santo	40	35	30	-9	3.1	3.2	3.4
Rio Grande do Norte	58	54	48	-9	2.6	2.6	2.8
Sergipe	60	55	51	-9	2.8	2.6	2.9
Roraima	30	25	21	-9	3.2	3.1	3.5
Pernambuco	59	55	51	-8	2.7	2.7	3.0
Ceará	44	41	36	-8	3.0	3.1	3.4
Rio Grande do Sul	42	38	34	-8	3.4	3.4	3.6
Amazonas	59	55	51	-7	2.3	2.8	3.2
Goiás	49	47	42	-7	2.9	2.8	3.1
Maranhão	56	54	51	-6	2.4	2.8	3.0
Amapá	49	47	44	-5	2.7	2.7	2.8
Bahia	42	40	37	-5	2.7	2.8	3.1
Paraná	44	43	39	-5	3.3	3.7	3.9
São Paulo	46	45	44	-3	3.3	3.4	3.6
Brasil	**49**	**46**	**42**	**-8**	**3.0**	**3.2**	**3.4**

Source: Censo Escolar (2005, 2007, 2009).

Note: Night shift classes are those that start at 5:00 p.m. or later (INEP definition). Enrollment and IDEB figures are for students in state schools in Ensino Medio.

Figure 6.5. Father's Educational Background for Prospective Teachers and Students Pursuing Other Careers

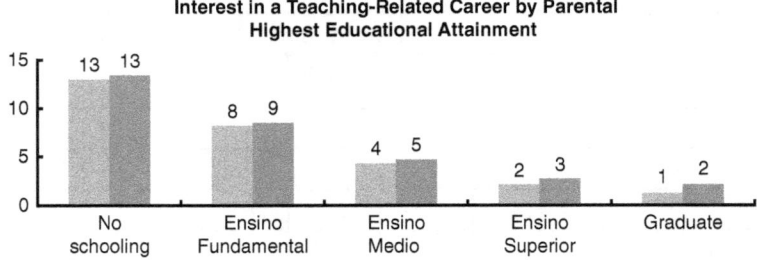

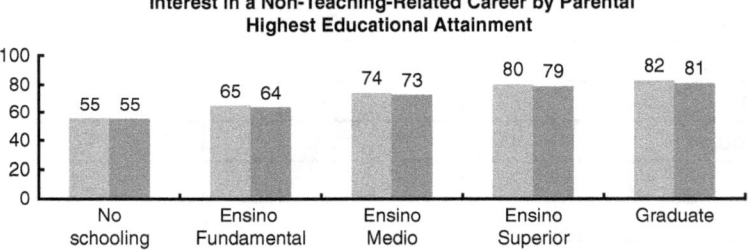

Source: National Secondary Education Exit Exam (ENEM) (2008).

Figure 6.6. Distribution of Years of Education Completed According to Household Income, 2009

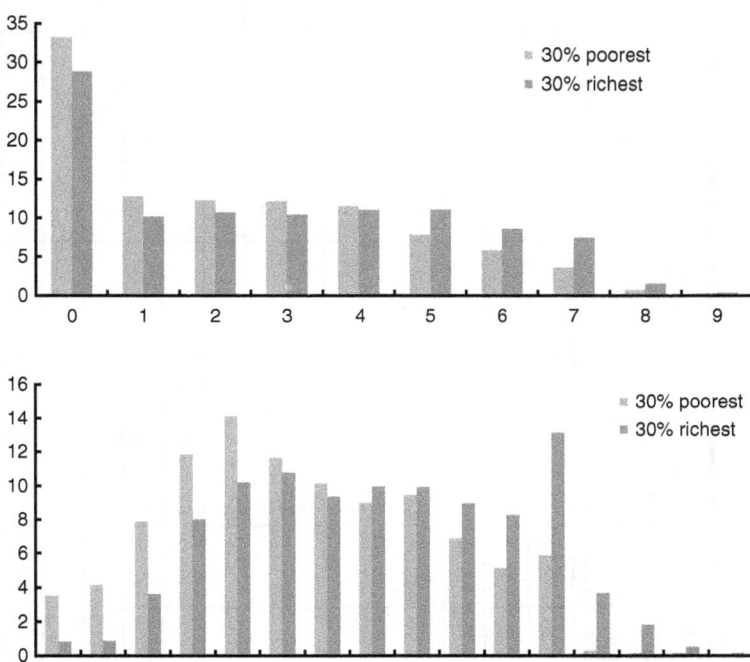

Source: PNAD (2009).

Note: For population aged 15–25 years who still live with their parents.

Table 6.8. SAEB/Prova Brasil Scores: Percentage Improvement in Basic Education by State, 2005/2007 to 2009 (Public Schools only)

States	4th Grade				8th Grade				3rd Year of Secondary Education			
	Math		Portuguese		Math		Portuguese		Math		Portuguese	
	2005/2009	2007/2009	2005/2009	2007/2009	2005/2009	2007/2009	2005/2009	2007/2009	2005/2009	2007/2009	2005/2009	2007/2009
Acre	13.7	5.6	7.0	4.8	4.7	0.4	4.9	5.4	4.7	0.3	7.8	3.2
Alagoas	12.8	1.6	8.5	1.6	4.8	1.2	6.9	4.7	-1.9	4.0	3.9	5.2
Amapá	10.9	3.5	5.7	2.7	0.7	-1.3	2.9	2.8	0.6	2.8	4.3	4.2
Amazonas	12.8	4.8	9.7	4.2	7.4	-0.5	9.7	4.1	6.2	2.7	10.4	6.4
Bahia	14.2	3.6	12.0	3.0	3.0	-0.2	2.6	3.0	2.9	2.6	10.3	6.3
Ceará	23.6	7.8	14.7	7.7	5.9	1.7	9.2	6.1	1.7	0.4	3.1	2.4
Distrito Federal	9.8	6.9	6.8	5.2	0.6	-0.4	2.3	2.1	-6.5	-7.7	-1.0	-5.5
Espírito Santo	11.7	6.7	7.6	5.6	2.8	1.1	6.7	4.9	3.2	5.9	5.4	8.8
Goiás	12.4	8.6	8.5	8.7	4.5	0.3	5.2	4.5	2.9	2.4	6.1	6.0
M. G. do Sul	13.8	4.5	11.0	4.3	6.1	1.4	6.7	5.8	4.4	3.7	5.8	6.1
Maranhão	15.7	0.9	8.7	1.9	4.6	0.3	4.8	3.9	5.4	0.7	9.4	3.2
Mato Grosso	14.7	5.3	10.8	5.1	6.7	1.5	8.2	6.1	0.0	-0.9	1.6	2.2
Minas Gerais	11.8	11.9	8.8	10.6	3.8	2.3	6.8	5.3	-1.0	-1.1	2.7	-0.9
Pará	13.2	4.0	6.9	3.9	-0.3	-2.2	0.1	2.2	6.1	5.1	8.6	8.6
Paraíba	14.2	4.7	9.9	4.8	5.6	1.7	5.8	4.6	4.0	0.5	9.5	4.0

Source: INEP/MEC.

States	4th Grade				8th Grade				3rd Year of Secondary Education			
	Math		Portuguese		Math		Portuguese		Math		Portuguese	
	2005/2009	2007/2009	2005/2009	2007/2009	2005/2009	2007/2009	2005/2009	2007/2009	2005/2009	2007/2009	2005/2009	2007/2009
Paraná	10.3	6.9	7.9	5.1	5.0	-0.4	9.0	4.1	3.0	0.9	6.0	4.4
Pernambuco	13.4	4.0	7.9	3.5	5.3	2.6	7.5	5.7	2.3	0.4	2.8	4.1
Piauí	23.2	5.7	13.6	5.6	7.1	1.6	7.9	5.3	2.0	1.3	2.9	4.0
R. G. do Norte	21.8	8.1	16.1	9.2	6.9	1.3	7.7	4.5	2.3	1.3	7.6	3.8
R. G. do Sul	10.9	5.2	5.9	4.4	1.1	2.2	3.4	4.1	-0.2	4.3	2.8	3.6
Rio de Janeiro	7.3	5.7	4.8	4.9	4.2	2.7	5.3	4.7	2.9	1.2	4.7	2.6
Rondônia	12.7	5.2	7.0	4.2	0.0	-0.6	2.0	4.0	3.8	3.5	7.2	6.9
Roraima	8.9	0.1	5.0	-0.2	2.3	-2.3	3.6	2.1	-0.7	3.7	2.3	5.5
Santa Catarina	11.8	4.2	6.4	3.3	3.1	1.5	2.1	4.9	-0.4	-2.3	3.0	0.7
São Paulo	15.0	8.1	7.1	6.1	3.4	-0.5	3.7	3.0	3.4	0.5	5.9	2.8
Sergipe	10.9	4.2	7.8	3.8	0.8	1.9	2.0	4.8	0.2	4.8	2.8	8.8
Tocantins	16.6	5.8	9.8	4.8	6.3	0.3	7.4	4.6	3.0	1.5	6.8	3.7

Source: INEP/MEC.

Table 6.9. SAEB/Prova Brasil Scores: Percentage Improvement in Basic Education, By State, All Schools (Public and Private), 2005/2007 to 2009

States	4th Grade				8th Grade				3rd Year of Secondary Education			
	Math		Portuguese		Math		Portuguese		Math		Portuguese	
	2005/ 2009	2007/ 2009	2005/ 2009	2007/ 2009	2005/ 2009	2007/ 2009	2005/ 2009	2007/ 2009	2005/ 2009	2007/ 2009	2005/ 2009	2007/ 2009
Acre	17.0	7.4	11.1	7.3	5.9	1.7	5.8	6.6	4.66	0.30	7.77	3.21
Alagoas	6.4	0.2	1.7	0.3	1.8	0.6	5.5	4.5	-1.87	4.02	3.90	5.19
Amapá	14.1	6.0	9.2	5.5	1.2	0.4	3.9	4.5	0.57	2.84	4.27	4.23
Amazonas	16.5	8.0	14.6	6.7	9.7	1.2	12.1	5.6	6.19	2.74	10.44	6.41
Bahia	11.2	4.2	6.1	4.2	1.7	-0.2	0.7	2.7	2.91	2.61	10.31	6.33
Ceará	21.7	6.1	10.7	8.6	9.0	1.8	13.6	6.8	1.74	0.43	3.07	2.44
Distrito Federal	11.4	7.0	8.5	5.1	0.4	-0.5	2.8	2.5	-6.55	-7.74	-0.97	-5.52
Espírito Santo	14.0	8.3	5.5	6.0	-0.6	1.0	6.0	4.8	3.15	5.90	5.44	8.79
Goiás	15.7	9.2	14.3	9.5	3.9	-0.4	4.3	4.3	2.87	2.41	6.10	6.02
M. G. do Sul	14.3	6.8	11.5	6.4	6.2	1.0	6.6	5.5	4.40	3.69	5.80	6.08
Maranhão	10.3	1.9	2.8	1.9	3.1	0.2	4.6	4.4	5.44	0.65	9.39	3.16
Mato Grosso	13.2	4.4	10.3	4.2	5.6	1.5	8.2	6.5	0.04	-0.91	1.57	2.24
Minas Gerais	10.1	11.4	8.5	9.2	2.9	2.3	7.1	5.8	-0.96	-1.09	2.75	-0.89
Pará	12.4	4.3	4.5	4.9	1.0	-0.8	0.6	3.7	6.12	5.08	8.58	8.64
Paraíba	12.9	3.5	7.7	3.4	4.9	0.5	4.1	3.7	4.01	0.46	9.46	4.02

Source: INEP/MEC.

States	4th Grade				8th Grade				3rd Year of Secondary Education			
	Math		Portuguese		Math		Portuguese		Math		Portuguese	
	2005/2009	2007/2009	2005/2009	2007/2009	2005/2009	2007/2009	2005/2009	2007/2009	2005/2009	2007/2009	2005/2009	2007/2009
Paraná	5.3	3.8	1.7	3.2	5.3	-0.6	10.4	4.5	3.01	0.86	6.02	4.41
Pernambuco	13.9	4.7	9.7	2.9	5.6	2.4	7.2	5.8	2.35	0.36	2.82	4.12
Piauí	19.2	7.1	17.3	7.0	6.7	0.6	7.2	5.2	1.99	1.27	2.94	4.03
R. G. do Norte	17.5	7.5	15.7	8.9	6.2	0.8	8.1	4.6	2.34	1.29	7.64	3.84
R. G. do Sul	8.2	5.6	4.8	4.5	2.1	2.2	4.8	4.2	-0.24	4.29	2.80	3.63
Rio de Janeiro	10.0	3.7	2.1	2.9	8.1	3.0	5.3	5.4	2.87	1.19	4.74	2.58
Rondônia	16.2	7.1	8.8	6.2	3.5	0.5	4.5	5.0	3.80	3.47	7.18	6.88
Roraima	10.2	0.4	5.9	0.0	6.2	-0.8	6.2	3.6	-0.71	3.70	2.31	5.54
Santa Catarina	7.9	2.6	2.5	2.1	2.0	0.7	0.9	4.3	-0.36	-2.34	3.00	0.69
São Paulo	16.5	9.9	6.5	7.2	5.4	0.1	5.2	3.6	3.38	0.48	5.93	2.77
Sergipe	9.6	3.6	3.4	2.5	-1.0	0.9	0.9	4.2	0.22	4.79	2.81	8.85
Tocantins	13.9	5.3	9.4	4.7	6.8	1.0	7.3	5.2	3.03	1.53	6.77	3.71

Source: INEP/MEC.

Table 6.10. Distribution of Secondary Students by Age and Grade, State Schools, 2008

	Series 1	Series 2	Series 3
14 or less	96%	3%	1%
15	95%	5%	0%
16	46%	52%	3%
17	23%	35%	42%
18	21%	27%	52%
19	24%	27%	49%
20	30%	29%	41%
21 or +	38%	28%	33%

Source: Censo Escolar (2008).

Table 6.11. Share of Secondary Schools with high dropout rates, by State, various thresholds, 2008

State	All Schools			Public Schools			Private Schools		
Share of Schools with Dropout Rates above Threshold	40%	50%	60%	40%	50%	60%	40%	50%	60%
Rondônia	60.9	44.1	21.8	68.5	50.3	24.8	23.3	13.3	6.7
Acre	38.2	26.5	16.2	42.1	29.8	19.3	18.2	9.1	0.0
Amazonas	41.6	22.1	8.5	42.7	21.8	8.4	35.7	23.8	9.5
Roraima	45.4	23.7	13.4	45.1	24.2	13.2	50.0	16.7	16.7
Pará	34.3	19.4	9.1	35.9	19.1	9.2	28.6	20.6	8.7
Amapá	53.0	44.6	18.1	57.8	50.7	21.1	25.0	8.3	0.0
Tocantins	39.8	21.7	10.6	42.1	22.3	11.2	14.3	14.3	4.8
Maranhão	40.8	24.7	14.0	45.8	27.1	15.4	15.4	12.3	6.9
Piauí	42.4	23.9	11.9	48.4	27.6	14.1	18.5	9.3	2.8
Ceará	41.6	22.9	7.9	46.3	25.0	8.6	30.6	17.8	6.4
Rio Grande do Norte	32.4	14.1	5.4	34.6	14.0	5.6	26.2	14.6	4.9
Paraíba	34.4	20.7	9.0	38.7	23.2	10.1	22.2	13.7	6.0
Pernambuco	34.0	21.0	9.1	39.7	25.3	10.9	19.7	10.6	4.6
Alagoas	34.3	19.4	9.7	37.0	21.0	11.1	29.1	16.3	7.0
Sergipe	37.8	20.9	9.7	46.5	25.6	12.4	20.9	11.9	4.5
Bahia	33.1	19.2	7.7	35.1	19.8	7.6	26.4	17.5	7.9

Source: Censo Escolar (2008).

156 | Achieving World-Class Education in Brazil: The Next Agenda

State	All Schools			Public Schools			Private Schools		
Share of Schools with Dropout Rates above Threshold	40%	50%	60%	40%	50%	60%	40%	50%	60%
Minas Gerais	29.1	15.0	6.2	32.8	16.5	6.7	16.9	9.9	4.6
Espírito Santo	35.3	19.0	8.4	41.8	22.2	8.7	21.5	12.3	7.7
Rio de Janeiro	43.4	26.4	11.8	53.9	32.2	13.9	28.5	18.2	8.9
São Paulo	31.7	17.1	6.9	38.9	20.7	8.0	16.7	9.6	4.7
Paraná	28.7	14.9	5.9	29.5	14.6	5.9	25.7	16.3	6.0
Santa Catarina	31.1	17.5	6.1	35.6	19.7	6.9	15.1	9.7	3.2
Rio Grande do Sul	55.2	37.0	20.2	66.5	45.6	25.6	18.5	8.9	2.7
Mato Grosso do Sul	48.6	31.0	10.7	57.4	35.0	12.6	20.7	18.4	4.6
Mato Grosso	34.0	18.2	10.0	39.3	20.9	11.5	15.1	8.5	4.7
Goiás	26.7	12.6	4.4	29.9	13.0	4.4	18.7	11.6	4.4
Distrito Federal	27.1	15.9	6.5	28.0	18.7	8.0	26.3	13.7	5.3
Brasil	**35.5**	**20.2**	**8.9**	**40.9**	**23.0**	**10.1**	**21.0**	**12.7**	**5.6**

Source: Censo Escolar (2008).

Eco-Audit

Environmental Benefits Statement

The World Bank is committed to preserving endangered forests and natural resources. The Office of the Publisher has chosen to print *Achieving World-Class Education in Brazil: The Next Agenda* on recycled paper with 50 percent postconsumer fiber in accordance with the recommended standards for paper usage set by the Green Press Initiative, a nonprofit program supporting publishers in using fiber that is not sourced from endangered forests. For more information, visit www.greenpressinitiative.org.

The printing of these books on recycled paper saved the following:

Trees*	Solid Waste	Water	Net Greenhouse Gases	Electricity
2	61	963	214	1,000,000
*40' in height and 6-8' in diameter	Pounds	Gallons	Pounds	BTUs

www.ingramcontent.com/pod-product-compliance
Lightning Source LLC
Chambersburg PA
CBHW051930160426
43198CB00012B/2094